In this era of covertly evolving threats to our national and homeland security, and the complicated leadership that is required to manage the safety and security of our society, Dr. Mumm's intellectual and tactical prowess has given us that needed edge in this book. His work on applying the complexity leadership theory to managing drone airspace, in support of our local and global security affairs, is a paradigm for managing what can be considered an unmanageable political arena.

-Michael L. Hummel, Ph.D. Professor and C' ' D ----------t of
Criminal Justice, California Univ

D1518248

Dr. Mumm has attacked two extremely difficult problems at the same time: The government bureaucratic regulating methodology and the integration of drones into the U.S. airspace. He has woven together a brilliant methodology to solve both issues by using complexity leadership theory. The potential economic impact of drones is enormous and new ideas on how to use them commercially emerge every day. The FAA needs to make a fundamental process shift or be left perpetually at the starting gate. Congress and industry take note; the same leadership method described here could be used to help solve the most difficult problems facing your organization.

-Jay R. Snyder, Unmanned Systems Visionary and former Director
of Air Force Revolutionary Planning.

Dr. Mumm's refreshing writing points to all knowledge levels in everything he writes. He is the master of the professional and academic pen, taking complicated concepts and transforming his thoughts into clear, precise scenarios we all can understand. This important subject of drone integration applies to all of us in some way-from business to consumer marketing to our personal lives. It is a thought provoking and enjoyable read.

-Stephanie Miclot, DM, MBA, MFA, Marketing Vice President and Business Professor

The use of complexity leadership theory to help accelerate change in governmental bureaucracy is brilliant; let›s only hope that those leaders will take this book and its posed solutions seriously before something drastic happens with these out of control Drones. When I read through his work I knew this would be very important to our government and we can already see that coming to pass with the White House Drone incident.

- Dr. Bryan Forsyth, Colorado Technical University Professor

Dr. Mumm is a subject matter expert and scholar practitioner on drone technology. His new work should be a primer for anyone interested in better understanding the applicability of this modern day technology as an instrument for good; while offering caution on the misuse of the same technology for evil. Hopefully those in a position of policy making regarding drone regulation will read this carefully and listen to Dr. Mumm – for the precise reason that he is the guy who wrote the book on the subject!

-Dr. Bob Touro, Professor – CTU College of Business and Management

APPLYING COMPLEXITY LEADERSHIP THEORY TO DRONE AIRSPACE INTEGRATION

BY
DR. HANS C. MUMM

Motivational Press
LEADERS IN GLOBAL PUBLISHING

Published by Motivational Press, Inc.
1777 Aurora Road
Melbourne, Florida, 32935
www.MotivationalPress.com

Manufactured in the United States of America.

ISBN: 978-1-62865-202-4

CONTENTS

DEDICATION

"Once you have tasted flight, you will forever walk the earth with your eyes turned skyward. For there, you have been, and there you will always long to return."

–Leonardo da Vinci (Devaney, 2013, p. 1)

To my mother and father who taught me the value of hard work, dedication and a purpose higher than one's self in this life. A special dedication goes to my wife, Christina, for her support throughout the years. Without your talent, encouragement and love this book would still just be a "someday" thought and not reality. A heartfelt dedication and thank you goes to my family and friends for their unwavering support and encouragement over the years.

ACKNOWLEDGEMENTS

"The price of success is hard work, dedication to the job at hand, and the determination that whether we win or lose, we have applied the best of ourselves to the task at hand."

–Vince Lombardi

Over the last four years, I have received support and encouragement from a great number of individuals. Dr. Michael Hummel, Dr. James Tindal and Dr. Bryan Forsyth have been mentors, colleagues and friends. Their guidance and confidence in me has made this a thoughtful and rewarding journey. Jay Snyder, Daniel Goddard and Catherine Wiberg spent countless hours proofreading and listening to me talk about my research while helping me to hone in on leadership concepts applied to real world issues.

I would also like to thank the subject matter experts who took part in my research study for generously sharing their time and ideas. I have learned much though our conversations. Finally, I would like to acknowledge all the people who have worked with me and for me over the many years. You have all taught me lessons that I carry with me every day. Without your efforts, this book would not exist.

FOREWORD

Dr. Hans Mumm, an American patriot and lifetime promotor of creative problem-solving, offers in this book something rare in an era of rapid, superficial, toss-off communications. He offers deep, new thinking – on several topics of national and global importance. Mumm's central point is that we must open our eyes, and begin recognizing that non-linear solutions are imperative in an irreversibly non-linear world.

We live in an ocean of proliferating, incalculably interactive variables, their numbers and differentiation growing exponentially around us, causing us to rethink how we address the problems presented. This global state of play causes us to wrestle, too, with the accelerating pace at which problems appear. In this new world, decision making and policy leadership are more complex, often carrying higher personal and national stakes, and are not easy arts to practice. Old, seemingly time-tested ways of making decisions, including one-by-one variable identification and plodding moves toward consensus building, are often now instantly incomplete, inadequate, delayed and even dangerous.

In this well-researched, tightly woven volume, the author brings together essential elements of complex decision theory, different types of predictive reasoning, and some jarring technological facts – to make the point that we have to sit up, start looking at the world with new awareness of its complexity, and start taking stock of what this complexity means. Not least, national decision makers – in the public and private sectors – need to rethink how complex systems are designed, and how to more effectively manage the flow, growth, and shift of so many variables affecting so many aspects of so much of our lives.

As technology accelerates, proliferates, and presents new risks to society, we have to meet this mounting change, disorder, and insecurity with more creative and anticipatory problem solving. In the end, Mumm is an optimist, and with good reason. His military, civilian, aviation, policy, and practical experience lead him to apply – and to illustrate how others can apply – complex decision theory to the pace of technology's advance and risks that follow.

His well-sourced study is a deep dive into one vexing policy area, one that seems to continually stump public and private decision makers, testing the balancing act that maximizes technological advancement while preserving public safety. While this book pretends to be about UAVs, and does map a fruitful way forward, helping to disentangle the intersecting worlds of manned and unmanned sky-flying vehicles, my reading suggests that Mumm is onto something bigger.

This one policy area – defining how best to make our skies accessible and safe to all – certainly needs insights and dispassionate thinking of the kind this volume offers. And it will be of special interest, of course, to all those who worry about where the proliferation of UAV's is ultimately leading – to a more secure, or less secure, more convenient or less predictable world in the skies above us. But, this tailored study in complex decision making may have a far wider audience, one that reaches beyond the academic, legal, aviation and policy communities. The idea that underlies this tailored analysis of how to manage and lead in a wild world of proliferating aviation options and objects, is bigger than aviation or even decision-modeling in that world.

What the book chiefly aims to do is to focus on "the leadership challenge created by the requirement to integrate unmanned aerial vehicles (UAVs) into the national airspace system (NAS)," and how "the lack of UAV-related federal rules and regulations is a primary factor prolonging this integration," which in turn carries cascading implications for the country.

Nevertheless, what it also does is lift the cover on a vexing new reality, and thus presents a template for looking at other complex problems. Leaders of all kinds – and we are all leaders in one or another forum, if only in our own lives – must think hard about how to manage, balance and ultimately navigate and influence the ocean of data before and around us, and coming at us at ever higher rates of speed. His volume offers insights on how this overall societal phenomenon might be sorted out. Are there models in nature, science, history, or data analytics that might guide us forward in areas well beyond UAVs?

The answer that Dr. Hans Mumm has offered is, if only by allusion, yes. There are ways to manage and ultimately to lead in a world that seems at once incalculably more complex, less predictable, more insecure, and less given to solutions. And more, there may even be opportunities that lie ahead which enhance, rather than detracting from, our overall security and prosperity. Thus, just as UAVs may one day deliver more humanitarian aid than they do overhead ordinance or surveillance, there may also be ways to reconfigure and align any number of complex variable pools, and currents to better improve the lot of man, and make more predictable the processes by which we govern, lead each other, and under which we live.

As the author notes, "the days of discovering a problem and solving in one easy decision appear to be over," and "actions and reactions … now reverberate with the echo of intended and unintended consequences in a matter of minutes or days not years or decades …" complicating many aspects of life, but in this there is also a wave we may ride to a higher point on the beach, on many and varied beaches. Whether his solutions and complex decision leadership concepts will capture the public imagination, shake policy makers into some rethinking of traditional ways of doing business, or get integrated into the decision process for future UAV use, proliferation, and management I cannot predict. Too many variables!

However, I will say this. Reading this volume, with its thoughtful application of differing schools and lanes of scholarship to one another, leaves me thinking harder, wondering more widely and – in the end – becoming more hopeful that there is new thought afoot. If the problems are more "wicked," and they are, there is also a rising need for robust, non-linear thinking to fully understand, parse, and solve these problems. Dr. Hans Mumm has leaped into the deep end with this volume, and in the process has taken us a long way up the beachhead, helping us all get a better "bird's eye view" of what lies before us – and what we must do to conquer the uncertainties of our non-linear world.

Robert B. Charles, 2015

Former Assistant Secretary of State (under Colin Powell), former U.S. House Staff Director and Counsel (Speaker Dennis Hastert), former adjunct professor, Harvard University Extension School (Government Oversight and Cyberlaw), and current president of The Charles Group LLC, Washington, DC.

INTRODUCTION

The overall lifecycle of leadership does not lend itself to a simple definition or a defined timeline that anyone can follow. As much as society enjoys creating, all of the processes and technology to simplify our lives (although this is debatable), leadership deals with humans and humans are not that simple. The concept of developing leadership is older than the US Army, which celebrated its 240th year in June 2015. The need for leadership stems for the human need to be led. People have a desire to have direction, be inspired, be motivated to greater heights, not managed like a logistical shipment in a warehouse. A person wishing to be a leader must first understand that leadership is dealing in heartbeats, people who have emotions, needs, wants and desires. Consider Maslow's hierarchy of needs; a leader can provide some, however not all, levels of human needs. As "Maslow wanted to understand what motivates people. He believed that people possess a set of motivation systems unrelated to rewards or unconscious desires," (McLeod, 2007, para 1). If a leader (teacher) is to have the ability to develop future leaders (students) they must understand human needs in their many forms, allowing for the understanding of what the human needs and motivators are to the student. The teacher must adjust their own philosophies to best teach and align with the student without losing the essence and composition of their own core beliefs and philosophies.

A sustainable organizational structure should not dictate who the leader is and who the followers are. Structure is a desirable organizational attribute only if it services the organization and the people in it. All too often, an organizational structure is in place only to serve as a wage scale discriminator. The Peter Principle takes full affect and the marginally qualified tend to outlive the strong leaders of tomorrow. The organizational structure is literally upside at times. A leader must recognize the potential in people and develop the leadership skills as required. A person must want to be a leader, and not begrudgingly accept a leadership position simply because the monetary benefits in leadership positions appear to be more enticing.

This book examines the leadership challenges created by the requirement to integrate unmanned aerial vehicles (UAVs) into the national airspace system (NAS). The lack of UAV-related federal rules and regulations is a primary factor prolonging this integration.

This effort focuses primarily on the leadership portion of the solution and not the technological requirements. The research completed for this book discusses in depth in chapters 4-7 an adaptation of the complexity theory that offers a potential leadership framework for the government, industry, and academia to use for achieving the full integration of UAVs into the NAS. Due to the large number of stakeholders and the multitude of interrelated issues, a complexity-theory-leadership methodology was created and examined as a potential way to help the FAA accelerate their rulemaking efforts.

A word of caution is necessary for the reader when it comes to terminology in this field of study. The terms unmanned vehicle, unmanned air vehicle (UAV), unmanned air system (UAS) and drone are interchangeable to an extent although drone and UAV are differentiated by how the vehicle is controlled and the level of autonomy the operator has in relationship to the vehicle. These terms are used throughout the book and are defined in more detail as the reader moves from chapter to chapter. The reader needs to be aware that these terms are used in source material in many different ways, and some reference material may have used a term slightly incorrectly, however the reader should be able to follow along without much difficulty or effort.

The work is an adaptation of the author's original doctorate dissertation that focuses on United States UAV governance and leadership issues.

The United States is one of the leaders in the unmanned systems arena and includes the first significant use of recoverable autonomous weaponized systems in combat. Issues such as airspace, airworthiness, social issues, privacy issues, regulations, and the lack of policies, procedures, or governance are universal for all countries that are active in this technology area. The research completed for this effort makes use of the grounded theory methodology as it combines decades of written works and research along with interviews with subject matter experts and information gained from attending UAV related gatherings/discussions. The author uncovered significant FAA process impediments as well as some possible break through concepts that could work well with the complexity-theory-leadership methodology.

CHAPTER ONE

"Many people believe that decentralization means loss of control. That's simply not true. You can improve control if you look at control as the control of events and not people. Then, the more people you have controlling events — the more people you have that care about controlling the events, the more people you have proactively working to create favorable events – the more control you have within the organization, by definition."

General Bill Creech

COMPLEXITY LEADERSHIP

Leadership is a concept that many people study in an attempt to grasp at reducing the task down to a checklist with easy to understand concepts and "how to" charts. Anyone in a leadership position knows that leading people is not simple and checklists fail within minutes of moving towards an objective.

Why do people choose to follow one person or another? Why do we find ourselves drawn to a person? Is it really just charisma or does the leader possess qualities far greater and far deeper than that. The study of leadership is a lifelong school and sometimes the answers are not as easy as society might lead you to believe as leadership deals with humans and humans are not simple. One's ability to gain consensus from a group has many aspects associated with one's leadership ability from personality, to knowledge, to the trust members of an organization have for their leaders. In most organizations and governments, these attributes by default make this person the leader; however, this is not always the case in real life.

The pace of change in our world is occurring more rapidly than ever before in the recorded history of our civilization. With that change comes challenges and opportunities that present a new and different perspective of how today's and tomorrow's leaders need to think and operate. The anticipated (and unanticipated) ways in which businesses, governments and individuals behave while using technology such as UAVs and drones will be vastly different than the way prior generations have managed technological advances. In the absence of leadership, people have the option to create their own future or to wait for the elected leaders to come up with solutions. The drone industry has been patiently (or impatiently as time moves on) looking for a governance structure and framework to work within so the industry can move forward. The answer to this governance and leadership issue is an answer of inclusion and guidance, not of gauntlets and excuses.

Figure 1 - Unmanned Oversight - The Absence of Leadership

The forefathers of the United States understood that change is the only thing constant in the world and that adaptability and agility to change based on a new situation is key to the survival of democracy. The very notion that the government must continue its governance and oversight the same way today as it did fifty years ago is in direct conflict with reality of the world we live in.

The U.S. Constitution offers the notion that governments and citizens should not stand idly by if processes, procedures and norms are failing the people they govern. As the Constitution states,

"That whenever any Form of Government becomes destructive of these ends, it is the Right of the People to alter or to abolish it, and to institute new Government, laying its foundation on such principles and organizing its powers in such form, as to them shall seem most likely to affect their Safety and Happiness. Prudence, indeed, will dictate that Governments long established should not be changed for light and transient causes; and accordingly all experience hath shewn that mankind are more disposed to suffer, while evils are sufferable than to right themselves by abolishing the forms to which they are accustomed," (The Declaration of Independence).

Technological developments are growing exponentially. The concept of Moore's Law and his early observation is important as it illustrates that technological advances progress exponentially, not linearly. Why should policy and governance be any different? Why are we accepting of policy and governance that oversees and allows or disallows the integration of this technology to progress in a linear and authoritarian fashion?

The research and ideas presented here offer a new leadership paradigm, one that shows promise for today and will shape the future of tomorrow. The complexity leadership concepts illustrated in this book bring together and highlight a new way to lead groups, organizations and individual people, while anchoring it to the current challenge of integrating unmanned aerial vehicles (UAVs) into the United States' National Air Space (NAS).

This new leadership concept focuses on the issue of leadership and management as related to the integration and harmonization of UAVs into the United States' (NAS) (*AATT National Airspace System Operational Concept Description (Volume I)*). This leadership concept can be easily adapted to most if not all governance and oversight structures.

When examining the leadership and management of complex organizations, there are two different operational dynamics at work: leadership and management. Leadership, in this book, is the guiding of interactions of people, teams and organizations. Management in this context encompasses the oversight of inanimate objects (aircraft-UAVs), processes, and budgets. To lay the groundwork for this new leadership paradigm a quick explanation of complexity theory is necessary.

In complexity theory a system can be described as a collection of interacting parts which, together, function as a whole...This interaction is so intricate that it cannot be predicted by linear equations; there are so many variables involved that the behavior of the system can only be understood as an 'emerging consequence' of the sum of the constituent elements (Morrison, 2002).

A simple example of complexity in action is a large school of fish.

» The Problem: Self-protection of the smaller fish against the larger fish that want to eat them.
   − Vision: Schooling (Look Big)
» Philosophies: Move towards the center of mass
   − Move in the same direction of the fish near you. Sacrifice the fish on the outer edge as necessary.
» The actual school is emergent.
» Issues such as how to feed, how to find a mate, how close to swim to 'draft' off the other fish, etc. are propagated as the process is executed

Figure 2 - School of Fish

A complexity leadership method is:

» Typically, an excellent method to arrive at a solution set when there are several stakeholders and several related problem set issues.

» The leadership guides the process with a vision and a set of supporting philosophies.

  – It is important that the leadership gets this as correct as possible since it guides the process.

  – The leadership should keep it to the fundamentals.

  – The group dynamic may be modified during the process if the group loses site of the goal.

» Issue meetings held among the relevant stakeholders.

» Interim results shared with the other issue meetings.

» The result is an emergent answer set that can solve the problem.

  – It may not be readily apparent that the resultant answer set is sufficient until it is implemented.

- The minor details will sort themselves out in accordance with the answer set.

In a complex network such as ant colonies, beehives, etc. when one member is successful then all members become successful and this correlation is obvious as one looks at the complex network between the Federal Aviation Administration (FAA)/Industry/US and the worldwide economy.

Later chapters offer an in-depth discussion as it relates to leadership and the current FAA UAV challenge offering the reader a clear understanding of why the leaders of today must start to integrate a complexity style of leadership.

Ask yourself, if the only thing constant in the universe is change, then why do some people and organizations fight against the only thing that is constant in their lives? One reason is "organizational members are not likely to embrace change unless they experience some *need* for it. Embracing change typically means that people are dissatisfied with the way things are," (Burke, 1994, p. 214). As technology and the world around us change at an ever-increasing rate, policy and governance struggles to keep up with these changes. This gives rise to the question of whether or not policy and governance can keep pace in our fast-moving world. Is the issue dealing with how our governing bodies execute change? Do they need to reexamine their leadership and management methods to handle these radical transformations better?

Resisting change is not a new phenomenon. In the presented research, the investigator noted that the resistance does not appear to be the employees, contractors, aviation industry, or the research and development community; the resistance to organizational and performance-based change appears to be the leadership within the government structures. A 2005 Government Accountability Office (GAO) report states,

"FAA needs to continue addressing four key factors that, as GAO has reported, have historically contributed to acquisitions missing their original cost, schedule, and performance targets: (1) actual funding less than planned, (2) increases in projects' scope, (3) underestimates of software complexity, and insufficient stakeholder involvement," (*National Airspace System: Transformation will Require Cultural Change, Balanced Funding Priorities, and Use of All Available Management Tools: GAO-06-154*, 2005, p. 6).

The GAO continues to support the assertion that leadership and management resists change: "Efforts to transform FAA's workforce culture address an impediment to [Air Traffic Control] ATC modernization that GAO has identified, but will require a sustained, multiyear commitment," (*National Airspace System: Transformation will Require Cultural Change, Balanced Funding Priorities, and Use of All Available Management Tools: GAO-06-154*, 2005, p. 1). The GAO's report attempts to move the Federal Aviation Administration (FAA) away from the traditional linear, authoritarian thought process to a broadened cooperation and consensus process. "Some experts, and GAO's work, suggest that the FAA pursue near-term options, such as contracting out more services. After establishing a sound financial management record, the FAA could pursue options for greater financial management flexibility." (*National Airspace System: Transformation will Require Cultural Change, Balanced Funding Priorities, and Use of All Available Management Tools: GAO-06-154*, 2005, p. 14). This report includes a Workforce Culture Assessment and a Perceptions of Organizational Culture in the FAA's Acquisition Workforce and in other organizations. All of the information researched, analyzed, and provided indicates the "FAA's management must become performance-based... [and] adopt a performance-based management philosophy," (*National Airspace System: Transformation will Require Cultural Change, Balanced Funding Priorities, and Use of All Available Management Tools: GAO-06-154*, 2005, p. 77).

These findings by GAO or mandates from Congress may compel a response that attempts to "talk the language," but creates little substantive action in pursuit of the transformation. It is important for an organization to transform, not merely offer up incremental or transitional change. To transform means "to change in form, appearance or structure. Transformation in the context of the management of organization and system occurs first in individuals, and then in the organization," (Daszko & Sheinberg, 2005, p. 1). Transformational theory tells us that transformation is the creation and change of a whole new form, function or structure. To transform is to create something new that has never existed before and could not be predicated from the past. Transformation is a "change" in mindset. It is based on learning a system of profound knowledge and taking actions based on leading with knowledge and courage (Daszko & Sheinberg, 2005, p. 1).

As a complex, adaptive system the FAA needs to embrace enabling leadership philosophies that allow emergent leadership to flourish at the administrative and employee level of the organization. Outside consultants, complexity theory specialists and transformational theory experts need to be engaged in training all levels of the organization. Training at all levels is imperative. Often in government, important documents written without the mechanisms in place to implement the change never produce a transformation.

"The integration of UAVs into the NAS is so complex that a single organization, such as the FAA, does not have the ability to respond effectively to all sectors of this complex issue. The parties involved not only disagree about the solution, but they also disagree about the real nature of the problem," (Koppenjan & Klijn, 2004).

The days of discovering a problem and solving in one easy decision appear to be over. The actions and reactions of decisions now reverberate with the echo of intended and unintended consequences in a matter of minutes or days, not years or decades, keeping in mind that, "Government officials and public managers are encountering a class of problems that defy solution, even with our most sophisticated analytical tools. These problems are called 'wicked,'" (Roberts, 2000, p. 1). Wicked problems require a different approach in leadership style and execution. "A stakeholder collaboration ... [is one] example of how wicked problems can be approached, even under crisis conditions when power is widely distributed among the stakeholders," (Roberts, 2000, p. 16).

When the U.S. Congress passed the FAA Modernization and Reform Act of 2012 (FMRA), it required the FAA to develop a five-year plan to integrate UAVs into the National Airspace and "...is intended to guide aviation stakeholders in understanding operational goals and aviation safety and air traffic challenges when considering future investments," (Roadmap, 2013, p. 6). Congress passed this law because very little progress came from the previous FAA three-stage plan (2005). The first stage of this plan, scheduled for completion in 2007, was never finished. In November of 2013, the FAA responded to the FMRA by issuing the *Integration of Civil Unmanned Aircraft Systems (Team) in the National Airspace System (Saeed Nazari & Nejadsarvari) Roadmap*. "The roadmap is organized into three perspectives that highlight the multiple paths used to achieve the milestones outlined, while focusing on progressive accomplishments. These three perspectives—Accommodation, Integration, and Evolution—transcend specific timelines" (Roadmap, 2013, p. 6). The FAA's perspectives reflect their linear, evolutionary leadership style. It is their belief that

Integration of [unmanned aircraft systems] UAS into the NAS will require: review of current policies, regulations, environmental impact, privacy considerations, standards, and procedures; identification of gaps in current UAS technologies and regulations, standards, policies, or procedures; development of new technologies and new or revised regulations, standards, policies, and procedures; and the associated development of guidance material, training, and certification of aircraft systems, propulsion systems, and airmen (Roadmap, 2013, p. 7).

This prolonged linear approach could kill off the nascent commercial UAS industry. The October 2013 FAA draft air-worthiness document for unmanned helicopters lighter than 750 kg is a perfect example of massive overregulation. In 128 pages of regulations the FAA effectively, although inadvertently, insures that only companies with the capital of companies like Boeing or Lockheed Martin could comply; moreover, they would only do so if the government paid for all of the effort.

The FAA uses a pedestrian Certificate of Authorization (COA) procedure that can take months to process the simplest of waivers. Wenger (2012) focuses on this issue when he states, "We are so infected by the culture of our organizations that we lose awareness of it. Ask fish what they think of the water and they will say, 'What water?'"

The FAA has found itself with the square peg (UAVs) that it is timidly attempting to pound into a round hole (manned aircraft regulations). Everything the FAA has done regarding manned aircraft regulations has been authoritarian, linear, and evolutionary. The FAA persists in trying to fit UAVs into the current set of manned aircraft regulations with as little change as possible. A fundamental mismatch occurs because the design of most of the regulations is to protect the life of the people on board the aircraft. With UAVs, there are no people on board to protect. The only risk is to other aircraft and people on the ground. This creates a significantly different equation and regulatory perspective. For successful integration of UAVs into the NAS, the FAA will need a leadership process that can address potentially disruptive technologies and concepts that have multiple stakeholders and interactions. A complexity leadership style has the potential to accelerate the process and produce a high level of satisfaction among the stakeholders.

Complexity theory leadership recognizes there are not just two or three primary factors or stakeholders that need to be analyzed in order to develop an optimum solution. There are many stakeholders and a myriad of key interactions that all need to achieve a certain level of satisfaction. This makes it difficult for a single entity, like the FAA, to achieve a satisfactory solution in a timely fashion. Fostering teamwork and stakeholder satisfaction requires stakeholders and individuals to work in an organized fashion, striving for unity of all involved. Several other leadership and management styles or systems could apply, but the research supports a complexity theory style as the best match for this situation.

What are the leadership challenges that are evident to bring people together to have an intelligent discussion on this issue? Natemeyer and Hersey (2011) state, "Leadership is typically defined as the process of influence. Power is defined as the potential for influence. Power is the resource that enables leaders to influence people to do things they otherwise would not," (p.440). Leaders must use what power they have (which may be very little) in order to influence others in a direction. The leadership challenges can be vast: from dealing with unresolved past issues, to groups and individuals not seeing eye-to-eye on the best way forward, to regulatory, insurance, and legal issues that can hamper forward progress.

In examining the leadership issues associated with the integration of UAVs into the NAS, one must consider that "given the challenges of contemporary times with numerous perplexing issues, the work argues that complexity theory is equipped with the tools to grasp the complexities surrounding public policy issues," (Ozer & Seker, 2013, p. 89). One such tool is the network diagram. There are many forms of network diagrams. In complexity theory, one typically develops a network diagram that connects stakeholders to nodes that represent the issues that need resolution. In this model, stakeholders are only connected to the nodes in which they hold a stake. This allows for a complete investigation of each issue since it is connected to all of its stakeholders. Through interaction, negotiation and creativity, the connecting lines increase to a sufficient level of trust for that stakeholder. That level of trust is a function of the stakeholder's desires and the stakeholder's relative power position. That level is part of the negotiation. These unmanned aircraft lines of sufficient trust often will be significantly different in their numerical value from a manned aircraft solution. That perspective is the key to achieving an overall successful solution. "Mapping system behavior in the absence of mathematical modeling allows researchers to incorporate a wider and less formulated system context, such as soft issues," (Bezuidenhout, 2012, p. 1841).

In complexity theory, a key leadership function is to define a clear actionable vision of the desired outcome. To guide the process, the vision statement must be actionable. The vision statement allows for a series of philosophies. These philosophes facilitate the emergent decisions that make up the eventual solution. They are guidance, not a set of regulations. There is no set number of philosophies, but typically, they are relatively few.

When leading a technological change, one cannot remove technology from the process. Interwoven as part of the creative solution, the technology is the spotlight and acts as part of the catalyst for the change. Synergistic technological capabilities are every bit part of the potential solution, creating the sufficient level of trust, as are the derived rules and regulations. The technologies that make up the FAA's Next Generation Air Transportation System (NextGen) are fertile ground for cost-effective pieces of the solution.

Figure 3 - Flower Delivery by UAV

In 2013, the Association for Unmanned Vehicle Systems International (AUVSI), the leading trade group for the nation's private-sector drone operators, estimated that the commercial drone industry would create more than 100,000 jobs and generate more than $82 billion in economic impact over the next 10 years. The challenge with this estimate is that it is based on the government moving quickly to establish workable operating regulations and safeguards.

Two forward-looking companies, Amazon and Dominos, are serious about using unmanned aircraft to deliver their products in thirty minutes or fewer. "With [their] drones possibly taking flight in the not too distant future, Amazon is raising the stakes in the race for faster delivery.

Figure 4 - Pizza Delivery by UAV

Jeff Bezos [CEO] believes the company has no choice (Rose, 2013, para 113). The drone and unmanned vehicle industry is now growing so rapidly that news stories by the dozens are printed every week and new trade organizations, clubs and user groups are popping up every month in every city and state in the US.

The FAA states in their documents that, "Ultimately, UAS must be integrated into the NAS without reducing existing capacity, decreasing safety, negatively impacting current operators, or increasing the risk to airspace users or persons and property on the ground," (Roadmap, 2013, p. 4). The real question is not about the need for the integration; the real question is if it is too late for the FAA to influence the integration at the local level. Users groups are defining their own safety rules and flight patterns. Local law enforcement is powerless to respond to concerns about drones in residential areas and now drones are flying over the Whitehouse while the Secret Service is powerless to stop them. All of this activity has occurred in the 15-20 plus year timespan that the FAA has had to write the rules, regulations and integration plans. It appears that in the 15-20 plus years the issue has been around, the linear and authoritarian mindset of the FAA governance structure is not obtaining the goal of integration

DEFINING AN UNMANNED AERIAL VEHICLE (UAV)

There are a number of definitions to describe UAVs. The simplest definition is "an aircraft with no pilot onboard," ("Welcome to the UAV," 2013, para 1). While accurate, this definition does not provide a robust description of a UAV. The U.S. Department of Defense definition provides more detail. "UAVs are defined as powered aerial vehicles sustained in flight by aerodynamic lift over most of their flight path and guided without an onboard crew. They may be expendable or recoverable and can fly autonomously or piloted remotely," (Introduction of the Unmanned Aerial Vehicles (UAVs), 2013, para 1). The National Council of State Legislatures provides another definition: "Unmanned aircraft systems (Team), also commonly called unmanned aerial vehicles (UAVs) or drones, have many applications for law enforcement, land surveillance, wildlife tracking, search and rescue operations, disaster response, border patrol and photography among others," (Unmanned Aircraft Systems (UAS) Legislation, 2013, para. 1). This definition includes potential uses for UAVs, but it does not provide a clear description of the vehicle. Another definition states, "Today, the term UAS is used to emphasize the fact that separate system components are required to support airborne operations without a pilot onboard the aircraft," (Roadmap, 2013, p. 7).

These contrasting definitions show that the United States, one of the UAV industry leaders, is unable to describe a UAV succinctly, accurately, and consistently. To date, even the basic definitions within the industry are not universal. This lack of consistency in definitions highlights systemic issues within the unmanned and robotic industries. At the center of this issue is the industry's lack of a singular legislative focus concerning policy for drone testing, development, integration and deployment. This study will use the FAA definitions.

Unmanned Aircraft (UA): A device used, or intended to be used, for flight in the air that has no onboard pilot. This device excludes missiles, weapons, or exploding warheads, but includes all classes of airplanes, helicopters, airships, and powered-lift aircraft without an onboard pilot. UA do not include traditional balloons (see 14 CFR Part 101), rockets, tethered aircraft and un-powered gliders. Unmanned Aircraft System (Team): An unmanned aircraft and its associated elements related to safe operations, which may include control stations (ground, ship, or air-based), control links, support equipment, payloads, flight termination systems, and launch/recovery equipment. As shown in Figure 1, it consists of three elements:

» Unmanned Aircraft;

» Control Station; and

» Data Link" (Roadmap, 2013, p. 8).

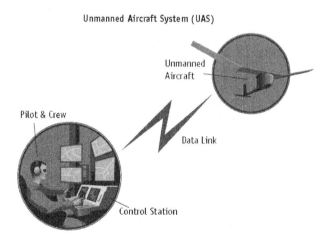

Figure 5 – Unmanned Aircraft System (Roadmap, 2013)

The term drone and UAV tends to be cited interchangeably although in reality these definitions have to do with how much autonomous behavior each vehicle has the ability to execute. A drone is generally operator controlled and the operator is actively engaged in controlling the aircraft throughout its flight. The drone can have hardware and software that can offer features such as stable flight, flight assistance and data links to the ground. A UAV has the ability for more of autonomous flight, meaning the aircraft, and if programmed in this manner is given a command (automatically based on event or by its operator) to take off, fly a predetermined mission profile and land at the appropriate time. The chart below offers the levels of autonomy as applied to this issue. Chapter 3 explores this issue further in reference to the FAA and levels of autonomy.

Levels of Autonomous Behavior

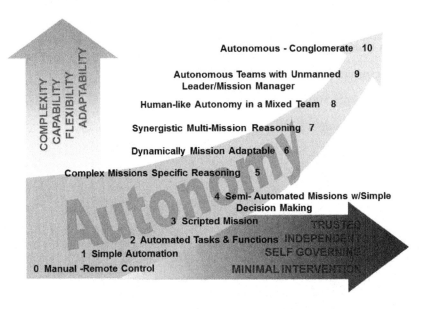

Figure 6 - Levels of Autonomous Behavior

The levels of autonomy also offer the ability for the aircraft a certain level of autonomy to make decisions in flight concerning the health of the systems and what is the best way to obtain the goals that its programming desires. An advanced example of this is if a UAV is programmed to track a ground vehicle, yet the UAV is encountering headwinds that blow it off course, the UAV can execute certain maneuvers that will allow it to catch back up to the vehicle even though this maneuver may not have been in the original predetermined flight path. Drone and UAVs are now in our daily lives; leadership must take an active role in shaping the integration and implementation of this technology.

The inability to agree to a common UAV definition directly affects the lack of leadership and policy. Contributing to the problem is the continuing evolution of UAV aircraft, ways of controlling it, communicating with it, using it, and the level of artificial intelligence incorporated into the UAV. Satellites and airplanes have extremely mature definitions. Without a uniform definition, common citizens and industry experts have difficulty confining and responding to UAVs. Only recently, the public and other decision makers have begun to glimpse at the revolutionary nature of UAVs.

A Brief History of UAVs

UAVs or drones, in one form or another, have existed since the nineteenth century. The earliest recorded use of an unmanned aerial vehicle for war fighting was on August 22, 1849 when the Austrians attacked the Italian city of Venice using unmanned balloons loaded with explosives (Naughton, 2002, para 1). Only recently, however, have advances in onboard intelligence, navigation, reliability, and sensors made drones militarily and commercially viable in large numbers. Initially, the industry expected that UAVs would have a low acquisition cost. That did not become reality. For example, the Global Hawk UAV was estimated by the Defense Advanced Research Projects Agency to the cost $10M per aircraft. Each aircraft currently costs $223M (Sia & Cohen, 2013, para. 2). Regardless of the price increase, the mission effectiveness and lower operational costs have made drones a cornerstone of the West's future military force structure.

According to a 2012 U.S. GAO report on the proliferation of UAVs between 2005 and 2011, the number of countries that possess drones rose from 41 to 76. Of those, 57 countries and 270 companies have created 960 unique UAVs (Wilson, 2013). In addition,

the majority of foreign UAVs that countries have acquired fall within the tactical category. Tactical UAVs primarily conduct intelligence, surveillance, and reconnaissance missions and typically have a limited operational range of at most 300 kilometers. However, some more advanced varieties are capable of performing intelligence collection, targeting, or attack missions. Mini UAVs were also frequently acquired across the globe during this period (Melito, 2012, p. 11).

Three nations are confirmed to operate armed UAVs. They are the U.S., the United Kingdom, and Israel (Heyes, 2013). It is unconfirmed, although widely suspected, that two additional countries have weaponized UAV programs. Armed UAVs will dominate the UAV market through 2025 riding the wave of their success in the war on terrorism. This success for UAVs is also due to several countries reluctance to use manned combat aircraft in many of the dirty, dull and dangerous flight roles that UAVs are more suited to execute without the risk of losing a pilot. The market for armed UAVs and military style UAVs is growing on a heavy up tick, as "[u]nmanned combat aerial vehicles (UCAV) will account for 34 percent of the market... The current UCAV market is estimated at $2.6 billion in 2015, and is forecast to reach $4.4 billion by 2015," (M. Peck, 2015).

CHAPTER TWO

"The revolutionary idea that defines the boundary between modern times and the past is the mastery of risk: the notion that the future is more than a whim of the gods and that men and women are not passive before nature."

–Peter Bernstein (Bernstein, 1996, p. 1)

A LOOK AT REVOLUTIONARY TECHNOLOGIES AND THEIR IMPLICATIONS

In July 1945, the first atomic bomb, code named Trinity, was detonated in the State of New Mexico ("The First Atomic Bomb Blast, 1945," 2003). The Allies then employed this technology in August 1945 to end World War II. Quickly after these events, the world's governing bodies understood that there needed to be strict governance and guidelines for the civil and military use of nuclear technology.

In 1957, the Soviet Union launched Sputnik, the first satellite, into space triggering the space race ("Sputnik and the Dawn of the Space Age," 2007, para. 1). Today more than 20 countries have active space programs launching manned and unmanned rockets into space almost every day. As of 2010, more than 52 countries had varying levels of recognized space programs ("Global Space Programs," 2012, para 19).

The United Nations (UN) clearly recognized the significance of the space race. They took action and created mutually agreed upon treaties, policies, and procedures to diffuse the potential for volatile situations. In 1959, the UN passed Resolution 1472 creating the Committee on the Peaceful Uses of Outer Space. This committee has negotiated and developed five international treaties that have been adopted by the UN General Assembly. In 1967, the General Assembly adopted the "Outer Space Treaty," formally titled "The Treaty on Principles Governing the Activities of States in the Exploration and Use of Outer Space, including the Moon and Other Celestial Bodies." In less than two years from the time that Sputnik changed history, the UN had a committee and a governing body in place. Again, the world's governing bodies understood that strict governance, policy and controls would need to be in place to control the proliferation and missions of space borne systems ("United Nations Committee on the Peaceful Uses of Outer Space," 2013).

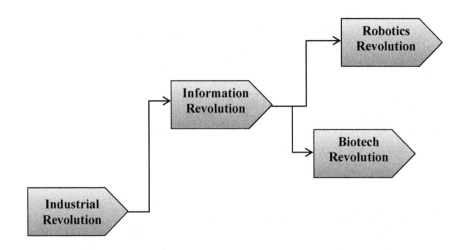

Figure 7 - Revolutions

Revolution is the labeling offered to describe technology and the radical change that it creates. People can misunderstand what revolutions are and where we are in history in conjunction with what revolution is taking place at any point and time during one's life. Figure 7 offers a glimpse of the past and where we are today on the revolutionary timeline. The lessons of the industrial revolution are well known. The revolution changed human history from manual labor to the mass production lines of today.

Some people believe that the world is still in the middle of the information revolution, although this is not true as the information revolution is in the past. The information technology space will continue to see gains in speed, storage space and capability, however, the revolution has moved on. The world is now in the biomedical and robotics revolution. Drones and UAVs are just a small part of this revolution. Leaders and lawmakers need to realize the importance of getting the governance and leadership piece of this revolution correct. Complexity leadership has the ability to guide both of these revolutions to the betterment of human kind. Using the present situation of cyber wars and cyber criminals, the past offers indications that the current path of linear and authoritarian leadership methods may not have created or guided the information revolution in the correct manner. It is time to work through and adopt a complexity style of leadership as the world moves through the biomedical and robotics revolutions and beyond.

UAVs and Robotics Emerge into the Mainstream

The emergence of UAVs parallels other transformational technologies that have changed the course of the human race. The emergence of both atomic bomb technology and space technology precipitated an industrial and policy response with guidance from world governing bodies. The UAV industry lacks this rapid response, even though UAVs and the robotics industries are rapidly changing our world. The UAV industry is a subset of the robotics industry. The UAV and robotics industry will affect every country, region, and city in the world. It will touch individual people's daily lives in ways that other technologies have not.

Why is it that UAVs, which have been around for more than 165 years, still have very little guidance, policies, or worldwide governance structures? Unmanned systems can carry lethal payloads and are tasked to do jobs similar to those of satellites, airplanes, helicopters, and balloons. However, it appears the world does not want to agree on how the technology could be used or proliferated. The bandwidth frequency that unmanned systems use remains unregulated. Although the Internet grew rapidly with little guidance, it operates in cyberspace. UAVs operate in airspace that is regularly occupied by manned aircraft and controlled by a wide array of regulations.

Why have military UAVs, or drones, proliferated so quickly? A primary factor is that the enemies of the West perceive that the West's strategic weak point is casualties, especially in foreign lands (Moelter, 2002, p. iii). Drones have decreased casualties and have the reduced the need to put people directly in harm's way. A second factor is that only drones can provide the type of persistence needed in the war against narcoterrorism. When enemy combatants refuse to wear uniforms and hide among the populace, it takes a great deal of observation to distinguish them from non-combatants. A third factor is that there have been few constraints on drone activity due to airspace and bureaucracy considerations. The FAA and European Aviation Safety Agency (EASA) have had limited influence on military drones. Rarely discussed is the largely untapped humanitarian use of drones, since the supporting governance and policy needed to support these missions has yet to be developed. This issue is discussed more later in this chapter.

This leadership concept presented here specifically narrows its focus to U.S. unmanned aerial vehicle issues. The U.S. is one of the leaders in the unmanned systems arena, and includes the first significant use of combat with recoverable autonomous weaponized systems. Issues such as airspace, airworthiness, social issues, privacy issues, regulations, and the lack of policies, procedures or governance are universal for all countries that are active in this technology area. The U.S. has neither prepared nor developed comprehensive documentation or plans to address the challenges presented by unmanned vehicles and robots on the modern battlefield or inside its borders. The reports that do exist are narrow in focus and are not widely distributed.

What happens when a new, truly revolutionary technology is unchecked, ungoverned, with only the human imagination creating structure in any form? Consider the Internet. In fewer than twenty years, the world has seen this technology blossom into what is now the lifeblood for many nations. This is an example of what can happen when a technology, created for the good of all humanity, proliferates without guidance or policies from the governing bodies around the world. Some of the great characteristics of the Internet are the ideas of freedom of information and the open information exchange, commerce, and worldwide communications.

What actually happened is a different story altogether. The governments around the world did not understand, and still do not understand, the true power of the Internet. They struggle to legislate against nefarious behavior and struggle even more to agree what these laws should include, how to impose them and what treaties would be intermingled within this framework. The Internet has created entirely new industries and new technologies, including ever-imaginative ways to wage war.

Cyber-attacks now number in the millions each week and there appears to be limited means for law enforcement or other government entities to keep up. There are few national and international laws against hacking and cyber-attacks and these laws are impossible to enforce. Cyber-crime accounts for 62% of all cyber-attacks as reported by Passeri in June 2013. "The Distribution of Target chart confirms the industry sector on top of the unwelcome attentions of the cyber-crooks, immediately followed by governmental targets…bear in mind that the sample must be taken very carefully since it refers only to discovered attacks," (Passeri, 2013, para. 5-6). This indicates that the cyber problem is growing and getting worse year after year. It appears that governments have yielded to the criminal element and they have lost the battle in the cyber realm. Governments appear to have no true effort in place to enact rules, laws or governance on a national or international scale that will positively affect this issue or attempt to interject basic rules of law enforcement into the cybercrime situation (Passeri, 2013).

The lawless underground and the exponential increase in cyber-crime should give the human race pause when it considers what unmanned systems can and will do to their way of life. Technology can be harnessed for good or for evil. Governing bodies help guide and direct technologies toward an agreed upon a set of parameters. Without them, some people will tend to move toward the darker side of the human spirit and put technologies to work for the purposes of evil, instead of existing for the good of all.

Although the UAV revolution started many years ago, it got off to a slow start. It is only recently—with the advent of critical technologies such as GPS and the miniaturization of key items that include inertial navigation systems, high quality sensors, and data links—that this technology has dramatically accelerated.

| CYBER SECURITY AND UAVs

UAVs have the option of partial or full autonomous flight. They must communicate with a separate control system to receive their initial set of instructions, deliver their sensor information and for any required changes during their flight time, therefore, if they are not utilizing encrypted signals, software, and other mechanisms, they become vulnerable to hacking much like a home computer. A 2012 article from the American Institute of Aeronautics and Astronautics (AIAA) stated:

"As these systems are unmanned, they cannot be directly monitored, and cyber-attacks can jeopardize the mission, the vehicle, and potentially lives and property. Given the potential severity of the consequences of security breaches, it is important to assess the vulnerabilities inherent in cyber-physical systems...[Due to] the increasing complexity of the networked embedded control technology, unmanned aerial systems (UASs) have become vulnerable to many cyber-attacks, and these vulnerabilities have not been thoroughly investigated," (Goppert et al., 2012, pp. 1-2).

The potential for a cyber-attack against UAV flight control systems, payloads (sensors) and ground control systems is as real as a cyber-attack against any other target. UAVs typically do not employ the same protections as a generic personal computer. A follow-up article in 2012 from the AIAA states:

"The United States Army, Air Force, and Navy have released plans for the increased use of UAVs, but have only recently shown interest in the cyber security aspect of UAVs. As a result, current autopilot systems are not designed with cyber security considerations taken into account, and are thus vulnerable to cyber-attack. Since UAVs rely heavily on their on-board autopilots to function, it is important to develop an autopilot system that is robust to possible cyber [attacks]" (Kim, Wampler, Goppert, Hwang, & Aldridge, 2012, p. 1).

UAVs and drones are susceptible to cyber-attacks and cyber issues. These issues are both in the front-end command and control systems and in the back end data correlation and storage devices that make up a UAV system of systems. The global cyber threat environment presents numerous persistent challenges to the security and integrity of the US government and private sector networks and information systems. Threat actors now demonstrate an increased ability and willingness to conduct aggressive cyberspace operations, including both service disruptions and espionage against US and allied defense information networks. There is an increasing concern due to recent destructive cyber actions against US private sector networks demonstrating capabilities that could hold US government and defense networks at risk. It is expected that for 2015 espionage against US government defense and defense contractor networks will continue largely unabated, while destructive network attacks capabilities continue to develop and proliferate worldwide.

The new automated non-physical world of cyber that controls unmanned vehicles and robotics, with its ability to be automated and programmed with predetermined responses, forces our thinking into new directions. The fact that UAVs in the future will become decision makers and not just navigators brings a new dimension to the process and the standard government policy methodology may not work to bind and control this type of technology and its uses.

THE WHITEHOUSE DRONE INCIDENT

The Whitehouse drone incident provides an excellent example of why we need to evolve and adopt a complexity style of leadership. At approximately 3AM on Monday January 26, 2015, a quad rotor drone flown by a person now known to have been drunk was flying over and crashed onto the Whitehouse lawn. This is one of those standup and pay attention moments for several reasons. If this drone was not flown by an admittedly drunk National Geospatial Agency (NGA) employee during his off-time hours, and was instead flown by one of a hundred different terrorist organizations that has vowed to do harm to the United States, this drone incident would have garnered more attention than it received.

This incident did not help the Secret Service who in their own right has been going through some rather difficult times that forced several changes to the Secret Service's leadership. According to a CNN article:

"The drone was believed to have flown over the White House residence after taking off in a neighborhood east of the White House...The Secret Service previously detained an individual operating a quadcopter drone on July 3 in President's Park, just a block from the South Lawn of the White House, according to a report filed with the Federal Aviation Administration. Another person was detained by the U.S. Capitol Police for flying a drone on the Capitol Hill grounds. And in October, a drone was spotted above D.C.'s Bolling Air Force Base, (Acosta & Diamond, 2015).

Another article by the RT Network, published on January 27, 2015, runs the headline of *Unmanned, unregulated & on White House grounds: Obama says drones need rules* and states:

President Barack Obama has acknowledged that federal laws for unmanned aerial vehicles – or drones – lag behind the technology readily available to consumers…Obama, speaking from India, told CNN that drones have magnificent potential, especially for commercial reasons, but overarching regulatory guidelines are lacking on this point (Unmanned, unregulated & on White House grounds: Obama says drones need rules 2015).

The president hit the nail on the head, however, drone guidance, rules, regulations and laws are so far behind it is hampering a market. Dozens of online and brick and mortar stores all over the US sell drones today. The numbers sold each week is staggering, yet the countries leaders cannot decide on how drones will integrate into the US airspace. The president is correct in that the genie is already out of the bottle; the best the FAA can do is work towards a compromise with some understanding that the next wave of technology is right around the corner, and start working towards governance and oversight that is able to be implemented and enforceable. The old ways of using the linear and authoritarian processes is what got the US and the FAA into this mess in the first place. History has proven that if you continue doing what you have always done and expect a different result the effort is guaranteed to fail.

Consider the idea of cognitive complexity; the notion that as a time-frame moves further out, an individual's intellect must disproportionately increase in order for the individual to interpret correctly the future state of an issue. This idea is why, for example, the US Government creates Program Objective Memorandums or POM cycles for the federal budget in 3-5, 5-7, 7-10, and 10-15 year timeframes. To support these goals, the government hires individuals with gradually increasing abilities in cognitive complexity to create these "future" budgets and plans. (Program Objective Memorandum, 2014).

Strategic thinking requires looking at the bigger picture and identifying patterns of emergent change in complex systems such as terrorism and being able to identify what constitutes a national threat. In an attempt to support senior level decision makers, many intelligent individuals have written reports on how terror organizations could be more complex and could start to work together (non-linear) as self-organized entities if they became united against a common enemy. These terrorist reports were created years ago and identified the underlying cause and effect of change versus focusing on the systems. However, many times senior leaders had and continue to have a difficult time operating in emerging complex environments. The leadership did not understand the value of the reports. Today, we are living the consequences of this continued linear, authoritarian mindset.

Homeland security and /or the FAA sustainability is based on the fact that no location or situation will ever be completely secure or completely safe. There is no way to mitigate all risks, only an attempt to control them or accept them. Security and safety will not be and cannot be controlled by a single concept or policy. Well-designed security/safety plans and policies are often created using an onion analogy with multiple layers, creating a robust response. The risk assessment plans and policies must outline and delineate the resources, funding, security posture, fallback and extraction plans for accidents, natural disasters, terrorist attacks or any other negative circumstance. The balance between safety, threat, vulnerability, response and resilience are managed with policies, governance and intellect.

Using complexity style leadership concepts allows for failsafe layers (flexibility) that can respond to and offer the best protection for unforeseen circumstances. If one layer fails, the subsequent layers offer additional protection, decision points and fallback positioning. In the end, the citizens will determine the success or failure in responding to policy requirements. The multiple layer of response in a complexity leadership environment creates a system of systems approach resulting in resilience and sustainability throughout and after the policy and governance is instituted.

THE FAA NEW RULES

Leadership means that sometimes one must stand up and endorse or change the decision an organization has just made or made in the past. The FAA late on Saturday night and into the early Sunday morning hours of February 15, 2015 over a three-day weekend "released a variety of proposed requirements for commercial operators to meet, such as passing a knowledge test administered by the agency as well as a federal security check."

Long-anticipated rules proposed Sunday will open an era in which small (under 55 pounds) commercial unmanned aircraft perform routine tasks — crop monitoring, aerial photography, inspections of bridges and cell towers, and much more. However, final rules are probably two to three years away (Lowy, 2015).

The FAA proposal offers safety rules for small UAS (under 55 pounds) conducting non-recreational operations. The rule would limit flights to daylight and visual-line-of-sight operations. It also addresses height restrictions, operator certification, optional use of a visual observer, aircraft registration, marking, and operational limits (DOT and FAA Propose New Rules for Small Unmanned Aircraft Systems 2015).

The proposed rule also includes extensive discussion of the possibility of an additional, more flexible framework for "micro" UAS under 4.4 pounds. The FAA is asking the public to comment on this possible classification to determine whether it should include this option as part of a final rule. The FAA is also asking for comments about how the agency can further leverage the UAS test site program. The upcoming UAS Center of Excellence is designed to further spur innovation as "Technology is advancing at an unprecedented pace and this milestone allows federal regulations and the use of our national airspace to evolve to safely accommodate innovation." This was stated by Transportation Secretary. Anthony Foxx (DOT and FAA Propose New Rules for Small Unmanned Aircraft Systems 2015). Interestingly enough, the proposed age rules to operate a drone, is seventeen years old, however, to operate a balloon or glider, pilots can be sixteen and be in training at any age. A drone appears to pose less risk and the pilot is under severe line of sight restrictions. The new proposed rules seem to be at odds with the logic of the old manned aircraft rules. The FAA appears to be set on attempting to take manned rules and policies and simply adapt them into the unmanned space. This logic will not work if full integration of manned and unmanned systems is truly the goal.

This admission/statement from the FAA offers the readers pause and a possible thought of empathy for the FAA as it struggles to create the governance structure for UAVs. This struggle is difficult to understand as Predator UAVs have been flying since the late 1980s for the US military and were integrated into the military operational mission space by the early 1990s. UAV use around the world for civilian and military purposes spans more than 15-20 years depending on what area of the world one looks at and when a particular UAV system is said to be operational.

Press releases with big headlines and little to know real substance only continue to harm the FAA. The FAA cause unnecessary frustration as the FAA attempts to get some heat off their administration when they announce that that they are releasing "purposed" rules. The issue is that these proposed rules still have a long road to go before becoming reality, if they ever even see the light of day after the press release and first round of public comment. If you are reading this right now and think that as the author I am being too tough on the FAA for these press release diversions consider this; in June 2001 the UK published DAP Unmanned Aerial Vehicle Operations in UK Airspace. In 2012, the UK released a fifth edition guidance document CAP 722 *Unmanned Aircraft System Operation in UK Airspace-Guidance* (Unmanned Aircraft System Operations in UK Airspace – Guidance, 2012*)*. Can we really blame the speed of technology for the UAV governance issue in the US? On the other hand, it might be time to embrace a new leadership paradigm that has the ability to leap frog the FAA from being wholly behind the eight ball to on par if not helping to lead the world in UAV governance.

WORLDWIDE NEED FOR UAV POLICIES

Although UAVs have been in use for decades, the world just now seems to be ready to acknowledge that comprehensive structured policies and doctrines will help the global neighborhood to be better prepared for working with unmanned and robotic systems.

The current complex set of international laws regarding what and where technology is proliferated along with the sophisticated integration requirements in dealing with UAV and robotic technologies discourages nations from addressing the issues head on. The solution set will not be easy and the coordination and collaboration that must occur will test the political will of the world. Borrowing from Henri Fayol's principles of management allows UAV policy to be flexible, yet hierarchical, striving for a unified governance and policy structure for the entire world to follow. The potential for UAVs and robotics to change human history is already upon us. It is now time to take back control of something that appears to be spinning out of control with a lack of leaders stepping up to make the difficult decisions that are needed.

Fayol discussed the "Unity of command - For any action whatsoever an employee should receive orders from one superior only...Just as the Biblical injunction advises - no one can serve two masters" (as cited in Wren & Bedein, 1994). What Fayol is saying is that dual command is a threat to authority, discipline, and stability and this is why there needs to be a single location for all governance and policy publication. Fayol also states that there must be a "Unity of direction ...one head and one plan for a group of activities having the same objective. It provides the coordination necessary for focusing...Unity of direction comes from a sound organization structure and is essential to unity of action" (as cited in Wren and Bedeian, 1994, p. 218). The world needs to agree upon one direction for governance and an overarching policy for UAVs and robotics, just as it has done with other technologies such as atomic energy. Both the atomic energy sector and the UAV and robotics sectors have the ability to do great things for humanity, but they also have the potential for great destruction and unknown long-term consequences.

The last principle borrowed from Fayol is one of "Subordination of individual interests to the general interest which is a plea to abolish ignorance, ambition, selfishness, laziness, weakness and all human passions" (as cited in Wren and Bedeian, 1994, p. 218). Fayol tells us not to place an individual nation's interest over all nations' interests, or that interest above humanity's general welfare as this would inevitably lead to conflict among all parties.

The lack of bi-country, multi-country, and internal country procedures and regulations has put a hold on commercially viable humanitarian UAVs and their operations. The U.S., Europe, and other countries have extensive road systems; however, around the globe there are many countries with very limited infrastructures. The UAV's ability to deliver medical supplies to and perform medical evacuations from remote locations throughout a country is generally well within a government's budgetary capability. UAVs are best suited for missions at the two ends of the spectrum: intermittent/standby operations and high-tempo surge operations. These attributes are also well suited to a variety of humanitarian missions.

SELF-ORGANIZED HUMANITARIAN MISSION

Putting theories and academia aside for a moment, one could ask can complexity leadership integrate into the real world issue of UAV governance; can a non-linear, non-authoritarian approach work? Self-organizing entities are creating humanitarian mission space for drones to do good for society. A linear and authoritarian process does not dictate the framework, the groups is self-organized and self-regulated. One such group is a new nonprofit group known as UAViators. This site http://www.uaviators.org offers experienced drone pilots a place to gather using social networking and (register) to fly and help with humanitarian missions. The site offers the individual drone user the ability to show to "the world how drones can save lives, not just take them!" The creator and founder of the site Patrick Meier wrote and published a book in 2015 titled *Digital Humanitarians* and UAViators is a natural extension to this work. *Digital Humanitarians* is based off the idea of how big data is changing the face of humanitarian response. As Meier states:

"The overflow of information generated during disasters can be as paralyzing to humanitarian response as a lack of information. This flash flood of information is often referred to as Big Data, or Big Crisis Data. Making sense of Big Crisis Data is proving to be an impossible challenge for traditional humanitarian organizations, which is precisely why they're turning to Digital Humanitarians," (Meier, 2015a).

The UAV's ability to deliver food and critical supplies in times of crisis can greatly expand the value and capabilities of governments and humanitarian organizations. Search and rescue operations and firefighting are two universal missions that save people and property throughout the world. UAVs are well suited to assist in monitoring dangerous situations from above or to extract individuals from a perilous situation.

How far along is this self-organized entity? UAViators boast a full complement of documents and governance structures for their members including links to:

» Research
» Pilot Roster
» Code of Conduct
» Operational Checklist
» Calendar of Events
» Directory of UAV Missions
» Directory of Organizations
» Directory of UAV/Imagery Software
» Training & Certification UAV Course

» Comprehensive Review of UAVs

» Using Non-Lethal UAVs in Conflict Zones

» FlipBoard Magazine - Non-lethal UAVs & drones (Meier, 2015b).

These links do not point to dead links or point to pages under construction. The organization has taken the time to create a governance structure that is robust enough to offer a safe yet flexible structure that can be employed anywhere in the world. This allows the organization to complete its stated mission and objectives, while being a model for other organizations to use in the UAV industry. The site also offers member's access to a law section that links to all the different countries and their individual legal framework (if the country has any at all) as it applies to the use of UAV in that specific country.

Merier offers communities of interest for inclusion of all people and groups, and the site is careful not to exclude individuals who are not specifically drone pilots. One of the communities is the *FlipBoard Magazine- Non-Lethal UAVs & Drones,* written by Sanjana Hattotuwa, which people are encouraged to follow the publication as it explores "[t]he use of drones for non-lethal, non-offensive purposes anchored to peacebuilding, peacekeeping, the protection and saving of lives, environmental conservation, wildlife protection and humanitarian aid," (Hattotuwa, 2015).

Patrick Meier appears to have understood the underlying truths of UAVs, that UAVs are a "truck" for hauling sensors and that it is the information provided through those sensors that create the value proposition. Meier is integrating the information into his existing big data networks that allows a first of its kind emergency response network and system of systems. Big data will continue to change disaster response and humanitarian response as the ability to access, sort and analyze large data stores becomes easier and more intuitive for emergency responders and the public. The use of big data for predictive analytics is just one narrow field of endeavor for disaster response and humanitarian response fueled by the desire and ability to gain a greater understanding of the world around us. The goal in gaining that greater understanding is not simply to have an appreciation for the subject matter; it is to further add to the book of knowledge for human kind and increase the efficiency and effectiveness for disaster response and humanitarian response.

Wisdom should be the product of data and information. A tremendous data and information overload will grow exponentially in the future. The disaster response industry's focus needs to be converting this information and data into wisdom. Past wisdom can help guide the creation of new wisdom. One method to aid in this creative process is to turn words and photos into a literal situational awareness pictures as humans are visual creatures and appear to be able to gain a more rapid and deeper understanding of a situation through visual means. People can integrate pictures quicker and easier. The specifics of how to accomplish this goal for the worldwide disaster response and humanitarian response is beyond the scope of this chapter.

Despite the amount of data, skilled analytical professionals and proven senior leadership, the disaster response and humanitarian response appears not to have an efficient means to identify and react to "breaking events" using all forms of big data. For the purpose of this chapter, we shall define a *breaking event* as a compilation of information, which when analyzed, is determined to warrant a report to prevent or mitigate current or projected impacts to disaster responses and humanitarian responses. The industry can leverage innovative self-organized entities such as *Digital Humanitarians* as recent advances in big data and information technology including analytical tools/models/applications, data infrastructures, modeling and simulation, and process to improve efficiencies to predict, monitor, and analyze information.

Currently, most disaster response and humanitarian response analysts use dashboards and timelines to capture information for a breaking event, which are ironically a representative "historic snapshot" of recent past events. The disaster response elements operation centers and selected analytic branches often spend time rewriting reports and reviewing several IT systems to track multiple reports to provide summaries of existing information to leadership. Often, for breaking events, the information utilized the most are reports that are months old and combined with current press articles. Therefore, most of these activities are focused on collecting past information instead of analysis and assessments based on newly collected information.

The ability to empower decision makers and analysts to be proactive during a breaking situation instead of being reactive, coupled with the lessons learned from past events would be a significant change in how the IC manages these events. The ability to leverage the existing IT infrastructure to provide efficient and effective analysis and "drill down" capability for use in pre-and-post-event activities could greatly change the response time for these situations. This new way of approaching breaking events would allow efficient use of personnel, funding, and resources to deter, detect and respond during the event, and assist in the recovery from the event.

Governments need to integrate citizens into the disaster response and humanitarian response enterprises. This includes the need to successfully prepare for all types of hazards through partnerships with NGOs and other private entities (such as *Digital Humanitarians*) to operate awareness and participation campaigns. The local government cannot do it alone; partnerships between FEMA, the Red Cross and state organizations should be strengthened with the goal of including private citizens and innovative self-organized entities into the enterprise (Homeland Security: Boom and Bust-A Troubled History, 2010).

The leadership issues addressed here is that policy, leadership, and management challenges continue to impede the integration and harmonization of UAVs into the National Airspace System (Saeed Nazari & Nejadsarvari, 2014).

CHAPTER THREE

> *"Complexity theory and chaos theory both attempt to reconcile the unpredictability of non-linear dynamic systems with a sense of underlying order and structure."*
>
> –David Levy (Levy, 2000, p. 69)

CRITICAL MASS

Organizations can be modified to be more innovative and adaptive through unique leadership approaches. The purpose of this study was to explore the use and employment of complexity theory as a leadership and organizational change management tool. This tool could allow the FAA to effectively lead the integration and harmonization of UAVs into the NAS.

The key to any UAV policy is in gaining a foothold and becoming mainstream in its ability to gain critical mass. This will involve creating a tipping point where the new concept or behavior is accepted as the norm. The concept of critical mass is when a small or limited number of people have adopted a new way of thinking or carrying out an activity; it remains and affects only this small group of people. A wave of changing behavior is created when other people and organizations connect with this new behavior and the behavior is accepted and adopted by large masses of people and groups with little or no outside influences other than the initial momentum or change being introduced into the system. Critical mass is what is currently occurring in the small UAV market with the benefit of assistance of regulations from the FAA. As the FAA continues to sit on the sidelines, UAV and drone user groups, individual owners and organizations are creating their own acceptable behavior models. The movement of these acceptable behaviors does not appear to be directly related to social media or to the internet. The movement appears to line up with the concept of critical mass, which is defined as:

"Critical mass is a sociodynamic term to describe the existence of sufficient momentum in a social system such that the momentum becomes self-sustaining and creates further growth. Social factors influencing critical mass may involve the size, interrelatedness and level of communication in a society or one of its subcultures. Another is social stigma, or the possibility of public advocacy due to such a factor. Critical mass may be closer to majority consensus in political circles, where the most effective position is more often that held by the majority of people in society. In this sense, small changes in public consensus can bring about swift changes in political consensus, due to the majority-dependent effectiveness of certain ideas as tools of political debate. Critical mass is a concept used in a variety of contexts, including physics, group dynamics, politics, public opinion, and technology," (Tipping Point-The 100th Monkey Effect-Critical Mass 2015).

An interesting example of critical mass is in the discussion of the hundredth monkey phenomenon in which a learned behavior spreads quickly (some claim instantaneously) from one group of monkeys to all related monkeys once a critical number has been reached. The story behind this critical mass phenomenon originated with Lawrence Blair and Lyall Watson when they claimed that it was the observation of Japanese scientists. These scientists aresaid to have observed that some of these monkeys learned to wash sweet potatoes and gradually this new behavior spread through the younger generation of monkeys, creating critical mass and through observation and repetition the new behavior was adopted as the norm to all of monkeys. Watson then claimed that the researchers observed that once a critical number (critical mass) of monkeys had been reached—the so-called hundredth monkey—the previously learned behavior instantly spread across the water to monkeys on nearby islands (Tipping Point-The 100th Monkey Effect-Critical Mass, 2015).

In the UAV and drone policy discussion, critical mass is on the cusp of being achieved as a large enough number for adopters to innovate a social system so and the rate of adoption becomes self-sustaining. Generalizing this idea to all species, including humans, offers the idea that once critical mass is achieved (at this point in the UAV discussion this is an unknown number) the instantaneous spreading of an idea or the acceptance of behavior is valid for everyone (the remainder of a population). Reaching critical mass within society will also be similar. Once a certain number of people or organizations has heard of the new idea or learned the new behavior, it will become the new accepted norm. This growth and innovation is created without FAA guidance or interference. Drone user groups and other organizations are creating their own flight and safety guidelines. The difficulty the FAA faces is not occurring today, it is someday in the future as the FAA attempts to force UAV and drone users to adopt its policies—policies created long after self-organizing, self-sustaining organizations have created their own solutions. Here again is an example and an argument for a complexity style of leadership. The use of non-linear, non-authoritarian methods is already in place; the cry for abandoning the old system of governance through linear and authoritarian methods will only cry louder as the inefficiencies of the old methods spiral bureaucracy out of control.

COMPLEXITY IN DEPTH

There are a substantial number of stakeholders directly linked to the issue involving the national airspace and the addition of UAVs; the environment is now more complex and dynamic than at any time in aviation history. Looking at a non-linear approach to leadership and management offers the opportunity to adapt the application of complexity to leadership and management. When contemplating pros, cons, and implications considered in this research, Ortegon-Monroy (2003) suggested that there is a significant incongruence between complexity and command control.

"At the level of the self-managed team, this was experienced through a management style that promoted "thinking out of the box" and "being comfortable with the uncomfortable," but at the same time using a command and control system to make them [stakeholders] part of this process of becoming a learning organization," (p. 391).

Ortegón-Monroy provide guidance in public management with insights of how complexity theory can be applied to the management problem. "A second broadly accepted insight is that phenomena do not develop only by external forces imposed upon them. Entities (in public administration) do not [only] behave according to laws or principles, but they have self-organizing capacities," (Teisman & Klijn, 2008, p. 288). Boisot and McKelvy (2010) chose to break down variety (stimuli and responses) described as "...Ashby Space into different regimes: *chaotic, complex,* and *ordered*," (p. 421). They use variety in this manner as a stand-in for complexity.

FIGURE 3
The Ashby Space

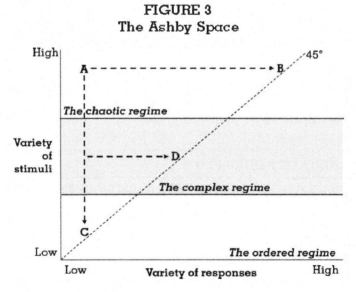

Figure 8 – The Ashby Space (Boisot & McKelvey, 2010 p. 421).

Saynisch (2010) argues, "Fundamental changes in sciences offer new perspectives for the management of complexity. Increased complexity in society, economics, and technology requires a new and suitable organization and management." He created a concept called *Project Management of the Second Order (PM-2)* (Saynisch, 2010, p. 21) as a potential solution.

Mowles, Stacey, and Griffin (2008) examine complexity as it relates to International Non-Government Organizations (INGOs) in their efforts to manage development in third world countries. Complexity " ...is a process of emergent planning where the plan itself and the assumptions behind it are subject to the same kind of reflexive examination as the work," (p. 816).

Bezuidenhout (2012) used a network-analysis approach to help handle complexity in a sugar cane supply system. Using "a cause-and-effect network-analysis approach could depict suitable key performance indicators as well as leverage points within the supply network....The analyses of the supply network [can] occur at a higher degree of abstraction..." (p. 1840).

Cooke-Davies, Cicmil, Crawford, and Richardson (2007) state that "the discussion about complexity in projects is simply one strand to the growing concern about the dominance of various versions of control theory, operations research, or systems theory in the studies of projects and project management," (p. 52). In their article, "particular attention is paid to those ideas that are directly relevant to the social complexity created by and among disparate groups of people who together make up the team involved in delivering complex projects," (Cooke-Davies, Cicmil, Crawford, & Richardson, 2007, p. 52).

Keith Morrison (2002) applies complexity theory to the school leadership problem. He developed a table that lays out the differences between conventional wisdom and complexity theory. Selected items from that table are reflected in Table 1.

Table 1 – Conventional Wisdom to Complexity Theory Mapping

Conventional Wisdom	Complexity Theory
Small changes produce small effects	Small changes produce huge effects
Effects are straightforward functions of causes	Effects are not straightforward functions of causes
Similar initial conditions produce similar outcomes	Similar initial conditions [can] produce dissimilar outcomes
Systems are deterministic, linear and stable	Systems [appear to be] indeterministic, nonlinear and unstable
Systems are fixed and finite	Systems evolve, emerge and are infinite
Universal, all-encompassing theories can account for phenomena	Local, situationally specific theories account for phenomena
A system can be understood by analyzing its component elements (fragmentation and atomization)	A system can only be understood holistically, by examining its relationship to its environments (however defined)
[Input] is reversible	[Input] is irreversible - there is a unidirectional arrow [of] time

(Morrison, 2002, p. 9)

A New Leadership Paradigm

The pace of change in our world is occurring more rapidly than ever before experienced in the recorded history of our civilization. With that change comes challenges and opportunities that present a new and different perspective of how today's and tomorrow's leaders need to think and operate. The anticipated (and unanticipated) ways in which businesses, governments and individuals behave while using technology such as UAVs and drones will be vastly different than the way prior generations have managed technological advances.

Technological developments are growing exponentially. The concept of Moore's law and his early observation is important as it illustrates that technological advances progress exponentially - not linearly. Why should policy and governance be any different? Why are we accepting of the policy and governance that oversees and allows or disallows the integration of this technology to progress in a linear and authoritarian fashion?

The dizzying pace of advancement does not offer long reflection time in areas such as governance or consideration for our environment as a whole. Change is and will continue to be dramatic, unfolding in ways that can make the governance and integration difficult in most cases. This pace of change appears to be unstoppable, and yet the civilization of today and the future will expect nothing less. Leaders will need to adapt to a new and different leadership paradigm than any that they have known previously and that will be the challenge that we all must face and strive to embrace.

LEADERSHIP KNOWLEDGE ORIENTATION FRAMEWORK

James Hunt in his book *Leadership: A new synthesis* illustrates his idea of a Leadership Knowledge Orientation Framework, not in the context of how to lead an organization per say, more on how one would use knowledge and understanding in the employment of leadership (Hunt, 1996).

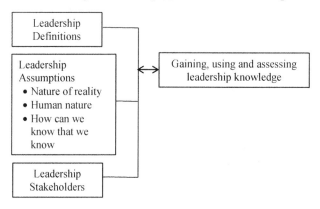

Figure 9 - Leadership Framework

Hunt is working to separate the specific act of leading (giving an order to an employee) with the deeper understanding and intricacies of leadership itself, or as Hunt stated it, as the "core notions in gaining, using, and assessing leadership knowledge (the knowledge-orientation aspects of leadership synthesis)," (Hunt, 1996, p. 43). Influenced by its purpose and stakeholders, leadership knowledge is the subject of study based on one's relational views of leadership definitions used by an individual or it can be situational dependent. This discussion is an expansion of Hunt's earlier chapters as the reality of human nature, one's own experiences, education and relationship to stakeholder groups and other leaders will influence how one gains and uses leadership knowledge in a given situation. The important issue here is a leader must learn and acknowledge these facts at a deeper level than simply reading a manual and give an order based on a hierarchical, linear, authoritarian feedback mechanism devised by others. The art and act of leading is more personal than that, and if a leader does not know themselves or understand the issues that surround the decision, it is difficult if not impossible to improve and be an effective leader.

Leaders must mentor and believe in the people they hire and they must be people with solid character and integrity (skills that cannot be taught, attributes either one has or does not) and instill in those employees the mission and vision of the organization. Leaders need to allow people to be creative, innovative, and take ownership of implementing solutions to hard problems with guidance and encouragement along the way, not micromanagement or the threat of humiliation upon failure.

The government tends to teach leadership methodology as something that is mechanical, hierarchical, linear, and authoritarian, which has and is failing, as time moves on. This leadership model has remained stagnant for many decades. Many "leaders" in the government still find it acceptable to yell, scream and throw things when a project does not go well, while not understanding that they are in charge and it is their leadership that caused the project to fail. If one does not fail at some point then the innovation envelope is not being pushed enough.

Tried and true is great for a cookie recipe, however in the world of unmanned vehicles, national security and cyber security, other countries (including America's enemies) are moving, thinking, adapting and attacking faster than the linear and authoritarian governance structure can react, so tried and true is a useless exercise at this point in time. Hunt's idea that reality as a projection of human imagination "are acts of creative imagination and essentially assume that an individual's mind is that person's world…leaders and followers are seen as transcendental beings who shape the world within the realm of their own immediate experience," (Hunt, 1996, p. 47).

Even the casual observer sees that if we are to cling to the tried and true passed that most government "leaders" are so desperate to follow as this make these unadaptable, non-flexible leaders relevant as a recognizable gauntlet. Surrendering the notion of change, the only thing that we can do is to accept the status quo with all its faults and watch the US fall further and further behind the technological realm and ability to offer governance and leadership in the world.

Studying the leadership of Colin Powell offers a reality to governing organizations as he states, "Organization doesn't really accomplish anything. Plans don't accomplish anything, either. Theories of management don't much matter. Endeavors succeed or fail because of the people involved. Only by attracting the best people will you accomplish great deeds," (Powell, 2010, p. 9). True leaders have the fortune and privilege of working with some of the greatest intellects and patriots of our time, and it is not by accident. One can build their leadership reputation to the point where people seek out specific leaders that they want to work for, as they believe in them. A true leader must engage people to the point they create job satisfaction that is more than just a paycheck and the work becomes a passion for the employee.

MICRO-MANAGEMENT

Micro managing may be the downfall of the policy makers in the long-run. So many talented people stand ready to help giving their time, talent and innovative nature hoping that the policy makers trust them. If policy maker's micro-manage then they will only get the results that they are dictating out to people and organizations. If the human spirit and the spirit of innovation is given the opportunity to grow, the policy makers will be amazed at the incredible results.

Micromanagement is a leadership style in "which the manager or supervisor closely observes and controls some or all aspects of employees' jobs. A micromanager might allow employees little or no autonomy in decision-making and will typically want to have insight and input into even small decisions," (Why Micromanaging Is Bad, 2011, para 1). In this case, defaulting almost all UAV integration efforts to the FAA will tend to see the FAA reverting to its micromanaging of the past. The UAV integration should not offer a "Back to the Future" mentality using the manned aircraft version of the policies and regulations without the benefit of a true understanding of how the new technology will change old paradigms. Integrating these new technologies will create new industries and new uses for UAVs that will render the generalization policies of manned aircraft as applied to unmanned systems meaningless and unenforceable as time moves on.

A collaborative effort means that you must listen to facts and ideas that are presented and evaluate them against the mission criteria and objectives of the organization. All too often your mind is already made up and there is no changing it, even though you forced a tremendous amount of time and effort on your team members to create a document in an attempt to convince and sway your thought process; this forgone conclusion wins out every time. In order to get where we need to go policy makers are going to need to be willing to accept advice and be approachable, and although policy makers may think that this is the norm for them, it is not how the general public perceives the issue.

This micromanaging linear thought process impedes if not destroys innovation from the communities, groups and individuals that the leaders and organizations are attempting to influence. Micromanaging using this linear thought process will simply not work in today's environment. The idea that micromanaging creates results a leader or organization could be proud of is questionable at best. The linear/authoritarian nature of micromanagement goes against our innovative nature as human beings. Larry Putterman offers additional insight as he states:

Five dangers of micromanaging:

1. Paralyzed employees

2. High turnover

3. Slow growth

4. Missed deadlines

5. Missed opportunities

Reasons leaders' micromanage:

1. Ego

2. Insecurity

3. Inexperience

4. Perfectionism

5. Arrogance – No one is as smart as they are

6. Ownership – The business is their baby

7. Deadlines

Keys to success:

1. Trust others

2. Delegate as much as possible

3. Set decisions that can be made without consultation.

4. Expect mistakes to happen (Putterman, 2013, para 1-4).

The ability to turn around a team or division that has been micromanaged is to bring a ray of sunshine and hope to the organization and to watch people who were micromanaged and nitpicked under other leaders shine under non-linear leadership. Learning the art of giving permission to grow, stretch and reach the next level through a non-linear, non-authoritarian style of leadership offers solutions, innovations and growth that the all too familiar micromanagement style does not and cannot offer. Using a complexity style of leadership offers teams the ability to learn from failure and come quickly back to triumph with success that is far beyond the poor results seen in micromanaged organizations. Technology moves too rapidly not to use complexity leadership as innovation in the real world tends to be tough teacher.

Maslow's hierarchy of needs offers the idea that employees, once they meet their needs, they seek a higher purpose or self-actualization. The employee does this in an attempt in their jobs, reaching their full potential and contributing to the overall success of the organization. Herzberg's two-factor theory also suggests that an employee that focuses on safety, fulfilling the lower rungs of Maslow's hierarchy, which will create job dissatisfaction, these actions don't create satisfaction per se. Satisfaction at work requires a different set of variables, including a feeling that work is valued or meaningful. Micromanaging is at odds with these classic motivational theories. (Why Micromanaging Is Bad, 2011, para 5).

The social and governance tipping point in the UAV and drone discussion with the lack of regulations, policies, and authorities may appear to the public as occurring spontaneously, yet this crisis of governance did not happen by accident. A complex chain of events occurred over several decades that included many deliberate calculated acts to create the current leadership crisis when discussing UAVs into the NAS. The idea of complexity leadership offers the ability to influence large groups without being authoritarian in nature, Indeed the FFA may not have to be prescriptive in the sense that complexity leadership allows people to be directly persuaded to change their behavior or act in a certain way by social contracts and people and organizations they readily trust.

The current use of linear and authoritarian leadership— being prescriptive, does not appear to be working very well and this is where complexity leadership can fill a gap. Policies and procedures often fail in conveying understanding, and on the contrary, the most effective and powerful actions are often singular statements of principle, not primarily intended to persuade at all. This is where complexity leadership shines, the new leadership paradigms must include all stakeholders, not discourage collaboration and innovation in the way current linear and authoritarian leadership styles do in today's world.

CHAPTER FOUR

Research Study-Managing the Integration and Harmonization of National Airspace for Unmanned and Manned Systems

PURPOSE STATEMENT

The purpose of this study is to explore the possible use and employment of the complexity theory as a new leadership and organizational change management tool, allowing the FAA to manage the integration and harmonization of UAVs into the NAS.

SCOPE OF THE RESEARCH

The scope of this research examined the U.S. airspace system in the context of incorporating UAVs. Worldwide issues were considered beyond the scope of the research, but they are introduced in certain areas and they may provide an avenue to expand on this research. International organizations, such as the United Nations, were also considered beyond the scope of the research.

RESEARCH ASSUMPTIONS AND LIMITATIONS

There were three assumptions that had to be identified at the beginning of the study. Those assumptions were:

1. Assume the FAA favors the use of the complexity theory.

2. Assume the manned pilots are in favor of research and development agreements to develop solutions.

3. Assume the UAV community is in favor of research and agreement to develop solutions.

There were also some limitations that had to be addressed for this study including: (a) the small number of UAV experts available to interview does not allow for a true random sampling, (b) the vast number of stakeholders precludes the principle investigator from interviewing them all, (c) the study was unfunded, (d) geographical coverage was restricted, and (e) the desire of the government stakeholders to alter their current leadership, management and policy practices.

RESEARCH QUESTIONS

For the research, the following questions were posed:

1. How might the FAA employ a complexity style of change management to integrate UAVs into the NAS?

2. Could the employment of a complexity style of change management expedite the integration of UAVs into the NAS?

3. What are the critical leadership issues impeding the movement of UAVs into the NAS?

THEORETICAL OR CONCEPTUAL SUPPORT FOR THE STUDY

"A system is complex when it is composed of a group of related units (subsystems), for which the degree and nature of the relationships is imperfectly known."

–Joseph Sussman (Sussman, 2000, p. 5)

The FAA has found itself with the square peg (UAVs) that they are they are timidly trying to pound it into a round hole (manned aircraft regulations). All of the manned aircraft regulations that the FAA has developed have been authoritarian, linear and evolutionary. When this authoritarian structure is overlaid on new, emerging technologies and markets, the resulting behavior is difficult to predict. The FAA persists, unsuccessfully, in attempting to fold UAVs into the current set of manned aircraft regulations with as little change as possible. A fundamental mismatch occurs because the overriding requirement for these regulations is to protect the life of the people on board the aircraft. With UAVs, there are no people on board to protect. For the FAA to succeed in integrating UAVs into the NAS, they must adopt a leadership style that can manage a multitude of stakeholders, interactions and address potentially disruptive technologies. A complexity leadership style has the potential to achieve a revolutionary solution to this complex problem.

Complexity theory of leadership/management recognizes that there are not just two or three primary factors or stakeholders that need to be considered or factored in to build an optimal solution. There are many stakeholders and a myriad of key interactions that all need to meet a certain level of satisfaction. This makes it difficult for a single entity, such as the FAA, to achieve a solution in a timely fashion since they require different problem solving techniques to address this broad range of stakeholders and interactions. By involving the stakeholders in an organized fashion, rapid satisfaction for individuals and stakeholders is achievable. Based on the research, a complexity theory style is the best match for this issue; however, several other management styles or systems may also apply.

RESEARCH STUDY SIGNIFICANCE

This study is significant to the aviation industry, academia, and the U.S. government because it holds the potential to develop a solution to a complicated problem. The study holds specific significance to the social science community as it provides a means to address leadership and management problems associated with new, advanced technologies that interact with a significant number of stakeholders. This structure allows

UAVs to be expeditiously integrated into the NAS to perform a multitude of missions including commercial, homeland security and humanitarian. This management structure appears to succeed because the leadership framework that embraces a non-linear design encourages disparate organizations to come together in a cooperative fashion and solve intersecting issues for the benefit of all stakeholders.

This research explored is an adaptation of the complexity theory that offers a potential leadership framework for the government to use in achieving the full integration of unmanned aircraft into the national airspace system. Examining this potential framework will explore a part of an overall solution, however, this study will not provide solutions to all of the challenges that make up an end-to-end integration of UAVs into the NAS. This research will explore and examine some of the potential pieces of the solution as part of the overall effort. The investigator selected certain nodes in the system to use as examples of how the process would function and move toward an overall solution set. This research was unfunded. The information cutoff date for the study was December 1, 2014. This information cutoff date is important due to the large number of articles published on a daily basis concerning UAVs, the UAV industry, military UAV use, and new UAV sensor systems.

CHAPTER FIVE

You never change things by fighting the existing reality. To change something, build a new model that makes the existing model obsolete."

- Richard Buckminster Fuller

RESEARCHING THE ISSUE-A DEEPER LOOK AT HISTORY

In order to create a solid future, one should understand the past as well as where issue stands today. As a first step in the research activity, the investigator completed a literature review into unmanned and manned aircraft flight operations with an eye towards:

» Researching complexity theory in change management

» Documenting current theoretical views and concepts on how to integrate the two systems

» Cataloguing and evaluating past research into the management theories and human factors that may help or hinder the integration effort

» Researching the social aspects of aviation and any possible negative stigma associated with the aviation culture

This review relied on a combination of government and contractor policies, regulations and reports, along with news articles, technical manuals, management concepts books, and homeland security manuals.

Although manned flight operations have been guided by the FAA since 1926 when the Air Commerce Act was passed (FAA, 2013, para 5) and the earliest recorded use of an unmanned aerial vehicle for war fighting was August 22, 1849 (Naughton, 2002, para 1); there has been little to no attempt to integrate the two flight technologies. Unmanned systems will change humankind, so why have we not integrated unmanned and manned systems before now? Upon reflection, priorities can sometimes be summed up by Maslow's hierarchy of needs and "one must satisfy lower level basic needs before progressing on to meet higher level growth needs," (McLeod, 2007, para 6).

This concept is based on theories of change that discuss the concepts of how an organization can implement planned changes versus forced changes. Planned changes include product lines or planned management changes. Forced changes include natural or manmade disasters affecting the company or the sudden stop of a production line due to the shortage of raw materials. The idea of a change model is the modification of the organizational forces that keep its systems of behavior stable. An illustration of the difference in change models is in the U.S. Intelligence Community. It had change forced upon it on September 11, 2001. Systematic and purposeful changes have occurred since those terrorist attacks. This is an important distinction to consider. Cummings and Worley (2009) stated, "Change that happens to an organization can be distinguished from change that is planned by its members," (Cummings & Worley, 2009, p. 23).

The literature on the subject is abundant if manned flight operations and unmanned operations are considered unique research topics. Conversely, the literature concerning managing the integration into air space is quite sparse.

The FAA states:

"In 1934, the Department of Commerce renamed the Aeronautics Branch the Bureau of Air Commerce to reflect the growing importance of aviation to the nation. In one of its first acts, the Bureau encouraged a group of airlines to establish the first air traffic control centers (Newark, New Jersey, Cleveland, Ohio, and Chicago, Illinois) to provide en route air traffic control," (FAA, 2013, para 6).

Since 1934, the air traffic control system in the world has been through many changes and upgrades, however, it has never undertaken the idea of having pilotless aircraft within its control space. In fact, in 2013 in an article titled, "Aiming for Seamless Skies," it appears the world is still attempting to create routes that are logical for manned air traffic operations with the goal of efficiency in flight operations (Paylor, 2013, p. 38). Albert Einstein said "We can't solve problems by using the same kind of thinking we used when we created them," (Einstein, 2005, p. 4) and this holds true for the current topic. A shift in perceptions is required to solve the problem.

The FAA predicts that by 2017 there will be as many as 10,000 unmanned aerial systems (UASs) in the U.S. skies (Dillow, 2013). The U.S. Congress, military, federal departments and agencies, as well as state and local governments, have been pushing the FAA to create a comprehensive set of regulations for all unmanned aircraft. Congress passed the FAA Modernization Act, Public Law 112-95, on February 14, 2012. This mandated the FAA to create policy and governance, including integrating UAVs into the U.S. airspace (Congress, 2012). The FAA acted in February 2013 by issuing a request for proposals to create six test sites for unmanned aerial vehicles. Fifty teams from 37 states competed for these test sites, affirming the strong demand for companies to capture this high growth business area.

The addition of thousands of civilian drones into the U.S. skies within a few years is fueling concerns that they could be used to spy on citizens. Legislative efforts are underway in several states to regulate unmanned aircraft. One small Colorado town is even weighing an ordinance to allow hunters to shoot down drones. Since 2008, the FAA has granted approval for drone use to at least 80 law enforcement agencies (Cornwell, 2013). Private industry sees the value in UAVs and the National Football League (NFL) and Motion Picture Association of America have reportedly both pushed the FAA to integrate the commercial use of UAVs into U.S. airspace (Cornwell, 2013).

The FAA has many significant similarities to a family run business. In *The Family Innovator's Dilemma: How family influence affects the adoption of discontinuous technologies by incumbent firms,* it states, "Incumbent firms…induce companies to strive for continuity, command, community, and connections, and thus alters the mix of constraints under which firms operate…it also aggravates critical sources of organizational paralysis, specifically emotional ties to existing assets and the rigidity of mental models," (Konig, Kammerlander, & Enders, 2013, p. 2). Another way of saying this is "Organizational members are not likely to embrace change unless they experience some *need* for it. Embracing change typically means that people are dissatisfied with the way things are," (Burke, 1994, p. 57).

The initial portion of the literature review focuses around the management of complex change. The first challenge of a problem such as the one facing how the FAA integrates UAV into the NAS is that it currently violates several of Fayol's principles. These principles include "(a) unity of command, (b) unity of direction, (c) subordination of individual interests to the general interest, (d) centralization, (e) stability of tenure of personnel, and (f) initiative as defined in *The Evolution of Management Thought,"* (Wren & Bedeian, 1994, p. 218). According to the *Simple Rules for Complex Change*, "First we need to recognize that successful change is best organized into three distinct phases, each having its own set of tasks and problems," (Johnson & Fredian, 1986, p. 47). The first phase is the preannouncement phase, then the transition phase and the final phase is the consolidation phase (Johnson & Fredian, 1986). According to Victor and Franckeiss (2002):"An organization must look at the macro issues first as stated in *The Five Dimensions of Change: an integrated approach to strategic organizational change management,* 'there are very few models or approaches that can provide organizations with a robust, integrated and pragmatic approach to enable them to understand the dynamics of the change process and then proactively drive the organizational change,'" (page 35).

Business process reengineering is used to assist in stabilizing an organization to succeed. It is essential that change be managed and that balanced attention be paid to all identified factors, including those that are contextual (e.g., management support and technological competence). Factors that pertain directly to the conduct of the project (e.g., project management and process delineation) are examined within the broader context of organizational change in a complex sociotechnical environment (Grover, Seung Ryul, Kettinger, & Teng, 1995).

In the *Models of Change Agency: A Fourfold Classification,* Caldwell discusses the important role of change agents and change teams. He states, "for the purposes of classification, a change agent is defined as an internal or external individual or team responsible for initiating, sponsoring, directing, managing or implementing a specific change initiative, project or complete change program," (Caldwell, 2003, pp. 139, 140). In using this definition Caldwell states "four models can be specified that encompass most of the existing research on change agency," (Caldwell, 2003, p. 140).

Table 2 – Four Models of Change Agency (Caldwell, 2003)

Leadership Models	Management Models	Consultancy Models	Team Models
Innovator (Kirton, 1980)	Adaptor (Kirton, 1990)	Action researcher (Lewin, 1951)	T-Group (Lewin, 1951)
Corporate entrepreneur (Kanter, 1984)	Empowerer (Lawler, 1986)	Facilitator (Tichy, 1974)	Composite group (Trist and Bamforth, 1951)
Transformational leader (Bass, 1990)	Developer (Pedler, Burgoyne, and Boydell, 1990)	Analyst (De Board, 1978)	Organic group (Meadows, 1980)
Strategic architect (Prahalad & Hamel, 1990)	Changemaker (Storey, 1992)	Process consultant (Schein, 1988)	Quality circle (Juran, 1985)
Charismatic leader (Conger, 1993)	Pathfinder (Beatty and Lee, 1992)	Catalyst (Blake and Mouton, 1983)	TCI (West, 1990)
Visionary (Bennis, 1993)	Change manager (Caldwell, 2001)	Counsellor (Feltham, 1999)	Task group (Beer, Eisenstat, and Spector, 1990)
Change leader (Kotter, 1996)		Exper (Cummings and Worley, 1997)	Guiding coalition (Kotter, 1996)
Change Campion (Ulrich, 1997)			Transition team (Kanter, 1999)
			Pilot group (Senge, 1999)

In *The Contribution of Learning Organization Principles to Large-scale Business Process Re-Engineering*, McAdam and Leonard identify the critical success factors (CSFs) in business process reengineering (BPR), stating, "These CSFs must be fundamentally understood if BPR is to be successfully implemented. The CSFs identified by the research methodology were: ownership, process issues, stakeholders, business, drivers, hierarchy, emancipation, communication, learning, and culture/power/politics," (McAdam & Leonard, 1999, p. 179).

Two concepts stand out for examining the social sciences in the complex world of managing the aspects of aviation. These two concepts both include the principle of phenomenalism—"Only phenomena and hence knowledge confirmed by the senses can genuinely be warranted as knowledge," (Bryman & Bell, 2011, p. 15)—and the principle of inductivism—"knowledge is arrived at through the gathering of facts that provide the basis for laws," (Bryman & Bell, 2011, p. 15).

Researching in the social science arena requires the ability to gather data by observing, surveying, calculating, collecting, and compiling large data sets from a population of interest. The researcher takes this information and places it against a given set of parameters, analyzing it not only for correct calculations, but also for utilizing the human curiosity and integrating it with the gift of intellect to create knowledge from the data sets. This knowledge can confirm or deny the hypothesis or lead the researcher to additional questions and lines of query not originally discussed or envisioned by the researcher's hypothesis (Creswell, 2009).

The capacity of any two systems to integrate hinges on the will of the people involved. All parties in this case demonstrate a high level of appreciative intelligence as described in *Appreciative Intelligence: Seeing the Mighty Oak in the Acorn*. They display "persistence, conviction that their actions matter, tolerance for uncertainty and irrepressible resilience and reaped the benefits of invention, creativity," (Thatchenkery & Metzker, 2006, p. 111).

The aviation community has used complexity theory in the past to solve finite, but challenging problems. Using a complexity theory model, Andreeva-Mori, Suzuki, and Itoh (2013) considered a new approach to aircraft arrival sequencing.

At present, the conventional way to sequence aircraft in the terminal area is to follow the first-come, first-served rule. Even though such sequencing is considered fair to all airlines and is associated with no increase in the workload of air traffic controllers, it is not always the optimal solution in terms of fuel burn and runway capacity... The approach taken is to provide air traffic controllers with a simple guideline which can help them determine the sequence without increasing their workload too much and whenever possible add up to runway capacity (page 200).

Using similar types of models, complexity theory and cognitive complexity in air traffic control will create better air traffic control pattern simulations for how to manage the integration of unmanned and manned aircraft into the same airspace.

NEXT GENERATION

A key portion of the literature review is the information relative to the FAA plans for the near future to modernize the national airspace system (*AATT National Airspace System Operational Concept Description-Volume I*, 2003).

Figure 10 portrays how the FAA breaks up the national airspace into different classes that have different sets of rules. This document is limited primarily to the examination of the exploitation of UAVs in Class E and Class G airspace. Class B, Class C, and Class D airspace are all types of airport terminal control areas. There is a lesser demand for B, C, and D airspace by UAV operators in the near term and this demand can be handled by exception. Large, unmanned, cargo aircraft would likely be the first significant demand in the terminal airspace.

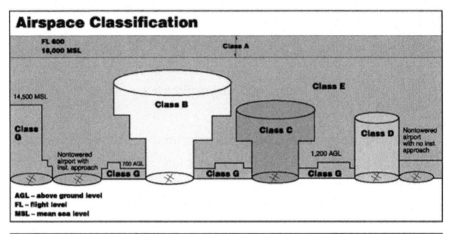

Airspace	Class A	Class B	Class C	Class D	Class E	Class G
Entry Requirements	ATC clearance	ATC clearance	Prior two-way communications	Prior two-way communications	Prior two-way communications*	Prior two-way communications*
Minimum Pilot Qualifications	Instrument Rating	Private or Student certification. Local restrictions apply	Student certificate	Student certificate	Student certificate	Student certificate
Two-Way Radio Communications	Yes	Yes	Yes	Yes	Yes, under IFR flight plan*	Yes*
Special VFR Allowed	No	Yes	Yes	Yes	Yes	N/A
VFR Visibility Minimum	N/A	3 statute miles	3 statute miles	3 statute miles	3 statute miles**	1 statute mile†
VFR Minimum Distance from Clouds	N/A	Clear of clouds	500' below, 1,000' above, 2,000' horizontal	500' below, 1,000' above, 2,000' horizontal	500' below,** 1,000' above, 2,000' horizontal	Clear of clouds†
VFR Aircraft Separation	N/A	All	IFR aircraft	Runway Operations	None	None
Traffic Advisories	Yes	Yes	Yes	Workload permitting	Workload permitting	Workload permitting
Airport Application	N/A	• Radar • Instrument Approaches • Weather • Control Tower • High Density	• Radar • Instrument Approaches • Weather • Control Tower	• Instrument Approaches • Weather • Control Tower	• Instrument Approaches • Weather	• Control Tower

*Only if a temporary tower or control tower is present is the exception.
**Only true below 10,000 feet.
†Only true during day at or below 1,200 feet AGL (see 14 CFR part 91).

Figure 10 – U.S. Airspace Classification
("The National Airspace System," 2013, para 4).

Any plan for UAV integration into the NAS must embrace this airspace structure. "In 2003, Congress passed legislation to create the Next Generation Air Transportation System Joint Planning and Development Office (JPDO) to transform the NAS to meet the potential air travel demands of 2025," (*National Airspace System: Transformation will Require Cultural Change, Balanced Funding Priorities, and Use of All Available Management Tools: GAO-06-154*, 2005, p. 3).

The importance of this transformation is that, "The aviation industry is critical to the nation's economic health, contributing about 9 percent to the gross domestic product. However, the ability of the NAS to accommodate increasing volumes of air traffic is limited," (*National Airspace System: Transformation will Require Cultural Change, Balanced Funding Priorities, and Use of All Available Management Tools: GAO-06-154*, 2005, p. 3). The FAA's next generation airspace system has its own cultural and technical challenges that are similar to the UAV experience. From a 2005 GAO study:

"According to participants, the key cultural factor impeding modernization has been resistance to change. Such resistance is a characteristic of FAA personnel at all levels, participants said, and management, in the experience of some, is more resistant than employees who may fear that new technologies will threaten their jobs. The key technical factor affecting modernization, participants said, has been a shortfall in the technical expertise needed to design, develop, or manage complex air traffic systems," ("National Airspace System: Experts' Views on Improving the U.S. Air Traffic Control Modernization Program: GAO-05-333SP," 2005, p. 2).

In *A Look Into the Future: Are we Ready?* Lynch outlines the basic plan for the Next Generation Air Transportation System (NGATS).

Aircraft in 2025 will rely on new avionics to "sense, control, communicate and navigate with increasing levels of autonomy…The air traffic controller would manage traffic flow rather than individual flights…intervention with individual flights will be minimal. Data link will replace voice communications, and automation will result in facility consolidation and virtual facilities," (Lynch, 2005, p. 48).

The FAA stated this concept in a different way.

While reduced reliance on human operators and analysts is the goal of autonomy, one of the major challenges is how to maintain and facilitate interactions with the operator and other human agents. An alternative statement of the goal of autonomy is to allow the human operator to "work the mission" rather than "work the system" (*Unmanned Systems Integrated Roadmap FY2011-2036*, 2010, p. 45).

Table 3 – Four Levels of Autonomy

(Unmanned Systems Integrated Roadmap FY 2011-2036, 2010, p. 45).

Level	Name	Description
1	Human Operated	A human operator makes all decisions. The system has no autonomous control of its environment although it may have information-only responses to sensed data.
2	Human Delegated	The vehicle can perform many functions independently of human control when delegated to do so. This level encompasses automatic controls, engine controls, and other low-level automation that must be activated or deactivated by human input and must act in mutual exclusion of human operation.
3	Human Supervised	The system can perform a wide variety of activities when given top-level permissions or direction by a human. Both the human and the system can initiate behaviors based on sensed data, but the system can do so only if within the scope of its currently directed tasks.
4	Fully Autonomous	The system receives goals from humans and translates them into tasks to be performed without human interaction. A human could still enter the loop in an emergency or change the goals, although in practice there may be significant time delays before human intervention occurs.

A key enabler of the NGATS is the Automatic Dependent Surveillance-Broadcast (ADS-B) system. The ground portion of the system is expected to be nationwide in 2013 ("FAA selects ITT for satellite-based ATC system," 2007). Aircraft would automatically pass their position to the ground controllers as well as the other aircraft in the vicinity. Essentially, the "ADS-B is being used to provide radar-like surveillance services," (Warwick, 2011, p. 68). The requirement of the precise location of an aircraft using a cooperative system is set out in the FAA's May 2010 final rule that mandates aircraft broadcast ADS-B information in most airspace by Jan. 1, 2020. Following up on this requirement, "the FAA achieved two of the biggest milestones in its ADS-B program in 2010: the go-ahead for nationwide deployment by 2013 and release of the final rule requiring aircraft to equip with ADS-B out by 2020," (Warwick, 2011, p. 68).

Work on the ADS-B has progressed. "In the U.S., nearly 400 ADS-B ground stations were completed and operational by mid-2012, with most of the rest — totaling more than 700 planned stations — expected to be up and running by early 2014," ("Preparing for an Emergency," 2013, para 13). Figure 11 depicts the ADS-B ground coverage as of 2012.

NOTE: Coverage areas and tower locations are appoximate, with network map current as of 5/31/2013. Depicts typical airborne reception at approximately 1,500 feet AGL. User's signal reception range may vary depending on receiver altitude above ground and any intervening physical obstructions to line of sight uplink.

Figure 11 – ADS-B Ground Coverage as of 2012
(Common Questions about ADS-B, 2012).

Supporting this change in the NAS, "the Air Transport Association, which represents the majority of U.S. airlines, sees ADS-B as delivering more operational flexibility at a fraction of the cost of today's radar-based system," (Hughes, 2006, p. 37). The ADS-B is cautiously supported when the National Air Traffic Controllers Association states, "The National Air Traffic Controllers Association supports the ADS-B concept but has technical concerns, such as overreliance on GPS, and doesn't want to see the radar infrastructure dismantled," (Hughes, 2006, p. 37).

Another piece of the Next Generation Systems is the en-route automation modernization (ERAM) which is now operating at 13 of the 20 FAA en-route control centers (Schofield, 2012). This is encapsulated by the statement, "ERAM technology is the heart of the Next Generation Air Transportation System (NextGen) and the pulse of the National Airspace System," (Crossan, 2003) helping to advance our transition from a ground-based system of air traffic control to a satellite-based system ("En Route Automation Modernization," 2013). Schofield echoed this sentiment: "ERAM is aimed at replacing the backbone operating system used in the FAA's 20 en-route centers. It actually predates the NextGen program, as the contract to build the new system was awarded to Lockheed Martin in 2002," (Schofield, 2012, para 8).

When thinking of ERAM, the reader should think of it as the control of the highways in the sky. According to the FAA website, "A flight from New York to Seattle with an ERAM flight plan filed by the user is checked for route constraints for the entire flight.... Information on the flight is available to all controllers regardless of facility location, helping coordination," ("En Route Automation Modernization," 2013).

Federal Aviation Administration (FAA)

The literature review also examined the FAA's current procedures, regulations, and plans for unmanned aircraft. According to the FAA's website:

"A UAS is the unmanned aircraft (UA) and all of the associated support equipment, control station, data links, telemetry, communications and navigation equipment, etc., necessary to operate the unmanned aircraft. The UA is the flying portion of the system, flown by a pilot via a ground control system, or autonomously through use of an onboard computer, communication links, and any additional equipment that is necessary for the UA to operate safely. The FAA issues an experimental airworthiness certificate for the entire system, not just the flying portion of the system," (FAA Q&A Unmanned Aircraft (UAS), 2013, p. 1).

The challenge presented is "regulatory framework to ensure UAS safety does not exist. UASs have had only limited access to the national airspace...a lack of airspace for testing and evaluating their products, and data, which could aid in developing regulations is scarce,"(Federal Actions Needed to Ensure Safety and Expand Their Potential Uses within the National Airspace System, 2008, p. 9). The GAO states, "Addressing the challenges of allowing routine UAS access to the national airspace system involves the efforts of several federal agencies and could require a decade or more of additional work," (Federal Actions Needed to Ensure Safety and Expand Their Potential Uses within the National Airspace System, 2008, p. 9).

According to the FAA, efforts regarding UAVs in the Alaska region are a challenge because the "approval of UAS operations and pilots will challenge current regulations for manned aircraft," (*Expanding Use of Small Unmanned Aircraft Systems in the Arctic Implementation Plan FAA Modernization and Reform Act of 2012*, 2012, p. 4). The FAA is moving forward as the "standard approach would be to use FAR PART 135—Operating Requirements: Commuter and on Demand Operations. However, this Part is not written with UAS [UAVs] in mind and many sections may not be applicable," (*Expanding Use of Small Unmanned Aircraft Systems in the Arctic Implementation Plan FAA Modernization and Reform Act of 2012*, 2012, p. 4).

Unmanned aircraft are also going to affect several of the ongoing FAA strategies and initiatives centered around increasing capacity on the ground at the airports, increasing capacity for airport arrivals and departures, increasing capacity during inclement weather, and initiatives to increase safety; especially as it applies to the aircraft accident rate (*FAA Flight Plan-2009-2013*, 2008). The FAA lays out its overall Next Generation Business Plan with a series of strategic initiatives, strategic measures, core initiatives such as Unmanned Aircraft System Research and a variety of activity targets. Unmanned aircraft will directly affect outlying areas of the aviation industrial base and tangentially affect several areas of the overall aviation industry, (*FAA Flight Plan-2009-2013*, 2008).

Unmanned aircraft need to fit in with manned aircraft and up to this point in time the FAA has chosen to closely adapt current regulations for manned aircraft to unmanned aircraft. Key regulations and their many sub-parts were reviewed, such as Part 91-General Operating and Flight Rules (Part 61, 2013), Part 61-Certification: Pilots, Flight Instructors, and Ground Instructors (How many chickens are there in the United States? How many eggs do they produce?, 2013), and Part 21- Certification Procedures for Products and Parts (The United States Meat Industry at a Glance, 2013). Part 21 covers airworthiness, type certificates, and production certificates. These certificates within Part 21 will have a major financial and schedule impact on the UAV industry and the ability to operate a UAV within U.S. airspace. Part 21 typically has a vast array of requirements that must be met. Every requirement is a design item that often influences the cost and performance of the resulting platform. An enormous cost driver is the proof that the UAV has actually met every requirement at the component level and the aircraft level.

The same issues present themselves in the small plane industry as typified by a couple of efforts, "The FAA has announced formation of a Part 23...a tier-based system so that small recreational airplanes won't have to be designed and certificated under the same regulatory requirements as heavier, more complex and higher performance aircraft," (Reorganize Part

23, 2011, para 1). A new Congressional effort titled *Small Airplane Revitalization Act of 2013* will reduce the burden on the small aircraft manufacturers by recognizing that, "the average small airplane in the United States is now forty years old and the regulatory barriers to bringing new designs to market are resulting in a lack of innovation and investment in small airplane design," (*H.R. 1848: Small Airplane Revitalization Act of 2013*, 2013, p. 2).

MANAGE ANY INCREASE IN CONGESTION

Any time you add aircraft to airspace you will increase congestion. The goal is to manage that increase in congestion appropriately. UAV operations in Classes E and G airspace should limit the initial congestion impact. The first impact on limited FAA resources would be by UAVs flown on an instrument flight rules (IFR) flight plan that requires air traffic controllers to monitor the flight and provide safe separation. The second impact would be increased congestion in Classes E and G airspace with other visual flight rules (VFR). Especially in the east and west coasts, there are several potential tools to assist in managing the increased traffic.

A sub-issue that will repeat itself often is the speed differential between the typical UAV and manned aircraft, however, the majority of manned aircraft in Classes E and G airspace operate at speeds that are similar to the typical UAV that would share that airspace.

USE THE NEXT GENERATION SYSTEMS TO FACILITATE THE PROCESS

Compatibility with the future Next Generation airspace technologies will simplify hardware requirements and make manned and unmanned aircraft more integrated. The use of ADS-B (in and out) equipment will provide a significant advancement in the ability of the UAVs and manned aircraft to maintain safe separation. The ERAM system could potentially provide a real time traffic and future route projection of other aircraft to

UAV operators via their ground station and an Internet connection. A two-way communication would allow the UAVs future route projection to integrate into the overall picture.

UAV Licensing Should Be Easy, Inexpensive, and Tailored

Licensing is important because it can set a basic level of understanding. This set of rules and regulations must be clear. UAV pilots also need to understand the issues that can cause license revocation for improper operations. Requiring private pilot licenses and medical requirements that are equivalent to manned aircraft, however, is expensive and often inappropriate; some UAVs are just above the toy level. UAV operators should have UAV licensure and learn the skills and knowledge that match their needs. Generally, UAVs automate most flight controls and navigation functions. They require little intervention. A medical problem with the operator does not mean the aircraft will fall out of the sky. It will fly its mission and return home. Most, but not all, can also land themselves autonomously. Since the operator is on the ground, a regular doctor's semi-annual exam would be more appropriate than a second-class physical done by an FAA approved doctor. Current licensing and medical procedures for manned aircraft create a significant barrier due to cost, time, and skills required. These procedures are inappropriate for UAVs and would stunt the growth of the industry. Worse yet, they might encourage unlicensed operations.

TACKLE E AND G AIRSPACE FIRST

The majority of non-military-only UAVs will operate in Classes E and G airspace in altitude and speed. UAV operations in Class A airspace initially will be fewer in number and always under IFR control. Operations in Classes B, C, and D airspace puts the UAVs in the airspace of airport terminal control, often over urban areas, with a lot of manned commercial traffic. In the near-term, there is little need for UAVs to take off and land from major airports. Many do not need a runway at all; those that do can operate from smaller fields with less traffic, private fields, or military fields. Classes E and G airspace separation requirements will generally be between the UAVs and light, private aircraft or propeller driven commuter airline aircraft. This airspace allows both IFR operations and VFR operations, both of which are conducive to UAV mission operations.

For greater understanding of the current issues and the proposed solution, it might be easier to illustrate the issue by creating a complexity network map. Different problems create different approaches to complexity network mapping. For this type of challenge, list the stakeholders around the outside. Create a series of nodes in the interior that reflect the key issues in creating the solution. Connect each issue only to those stakeholders with a significant stake in that issue. It is better to add connections later than to include a stakeholder who just adds to the difficulty in achieving a consensus. Typically, this network map will quickly show the level of complexity facing leadership. Figure 12 shows a readable portion of the complexity network map for the UAV integration challenge. During this investigation, the interviews examined a subset of these issues to help answer the posed research questions. Figure 13 displays a network diagram of the airworthiness issues. For airworthiness, there are seven primary stakeholders. You will notice that Congress is not one of the stakeholders for any issue. Congress is an outside influence on the system operating in the form of a loop that goes from each of the stakeholders, including the FAA, to Congress and back to the FAA via the stakeholders. When properly exercised, Congress influences the relative power weighting of the stakeholders with regard to the different issues. This loop is not expected to be perfect, but it may be necessary to prevent the singular mindset of "my way or the highway" type of impasse.

As one can see in Figure 13, not all stakeholders are relevant to every issue. Although Figure 12 makes the problem seem daunting, the issue-by-issue subset facilitates the collaboration process. With a complexity leadership style, the methodology of the collaboration undergoes a process change as well. Instead of traditional problem solving in which talk leads directly to action, multiple simultaneous loops here give way to an emergent solution.

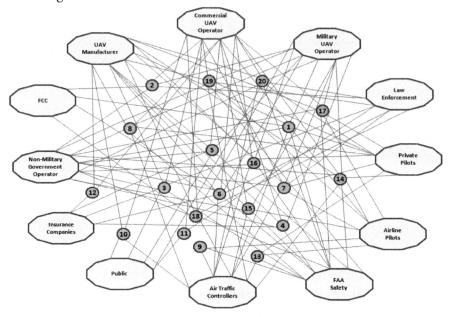

Key:

1.	Sense and Avoid	11. Privacy
2.	Frequency Management	12. Insurance
3.	Protection of People and Property (Urban)	13. Airway Congestion
4.	Protection of People and Property (Rural)	14. Next Generation ADSB
5.	Air Worthiness	15. Next Generation Info Network
6.	Licensing	16. Transponders
7.	File and Fly	17. See and Be Seen
8.	Required Equipment	18. Voice Communications
9.	Airport Terminal area congestion	19. E Airspace
10.	Noise	20. G Airspace

Figure 12- Suggested Complexity Network Map for the UAV Integration Challenge

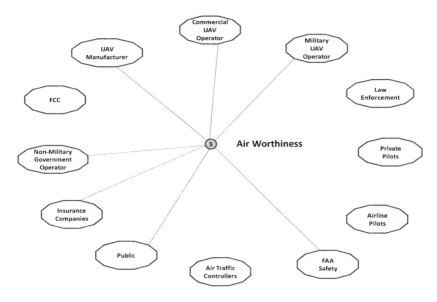

Figure 13 - Airworthiness Factors

A solution then maintains its relevancy by a continuing program of collaboration among the stakeholders. This process requires a creative engine in the form of a person or process to avoid a single stakeholder dictating the solution and to facilitate the emergent properties of the collaboration process. In 2004, the FAA executed a form of collaboration called Future Search to address the growing congestion on the airways and in the terminal areas. The key stakeholders participated in a short, whole-system meeting, agreeing to three important improvements. One was the "elimination of a decades-old 'first come, first served' policy of routing airplanes, enabling controllers to make systemic decisions," (Weisbord & Janoff, 2009, p. 356).

As the leadership changes from a low-order command and control system to a complexity style of leadership, a variety of organizational characteristics will need to be encouraged. An example of the organizational change is represented by Table 4, which was developed by Keith Morrison (Morrison, 2002).

Table 4 – Leadership Changes (Morrison, 2012).

Lower order	Emergent higher order
Organized	Self-organized
Mechanical	Humanistic
Directives	Empowerment
Hierarchical	Networked
Single leaders	Distributed leadership
Closed, dissipative system	Open, evolving system
Depersonalized	Relationship-driven
Demarcated and detached	Connected
Inflexible	Adaptable
Closed system	Open system
Restricted communication	Open communication
Enacted organization	Learning organization
Transactional leadership	Transformational quantum leadership
Passive	Active
Low-order thinking	High-order creative thinking
Censure	Feedback
Sterile environment	Rich environment
Private knowledge	Distributed knowledge

ORGANIZATIONAL MARKETING AND REPUTATION MANAGEMENT (PUBLIC RELATIONS)

As with any new endeavor such as the integration of unmanned and manned systems, the stakeholders must stay in lock step with the message that is delivered to their audience. The FAA and private industry as change agents will appear to the worldwide public as a single voice or a corporation. The way they convey, or frame, the message of managing the integration of unmanned and manned systems in a safe, logical manner will take coordination and careful management of the reputation of all stakeholders. Framing in public policy, why do it at all? Do the framers (influencers) believe that people are not smart enough to understand a topic or do they manipulate the issue for political or monetary gain? Lee and Chang (2010) claim, "How to frame the promoted public policy issues, advantageously has become an important part of political communication," (Lee & Chang, 2010, p. 70). The challenge becomes: are the framers promoting public policy issues for the education and understanding of the masses or are they using their craft to influence government agencies, politicians, business owners and the masses in a way that will benefit themselves?

This will not be the first time the government has had to "sell" an idea using a public/private message to shape an issue. The anti-littering campaign in the 1970s depicted a Native American Indian with a tear in his eye after rowing a canoe through litter-infested water and then watching people drive by and throw trash out of their car window. Leonard (2013) states, "Children and young adults watched it over and over, shared the faux-Indian's grief, and vowed to make changes in their individual lives to stop pollution," (page 244). The stakeholders in this case are everyone in society; the advertisement's purpose is to influence the young in order for a societal change to occur over time.

As stated in the article titled *Crafting Normative Messages to Protect the Environment:*

"It is widely recognized that communications that activate social norms can be effective in producing societally beneficial conduct. Not so well recognized are the circumstances under which normative information can backfire to produce the opposite of what a communicator intends," (Cialdini, 2003).

Literature abounds on the topic of how to build, maintain, and re-build a corporate reputation. The information is wide ranging and from many different countries. "The concept of corporate reputation may or may not exist in non-U.S. contexts. Even if a literal translation of the word 'reputation' exists, it may not have conceptual equivalence," (Gardberg, 2006). This literature abundance allows multiple points of view to evolve in the multicultural and multinational corporate worlds that now face businesses attempting unique branding and public perceptions in many different countries. The introduction of commercial and government UAVs into the NAS on a wide scale will involve a significant need for the concept of reputation management. UAVs, or drones as the media calls them, already have their collective reputation under fire. The successful integration of drones into the NAS is dependent on not only policy, regulations and technical advancements, but also significantly on the reputation of the UAV community. Wiedman and Buxel (2005) discuss the need for reputation management. The need is immediately apparent in their article's abstract: "The broad spectrum of potential for opportunity, however, cannot be purposefully exhausted without rigorous reputation management," (Wiedmann & Buxel, 2005, p. 145). The study offers a working definition of corporate reputation:

"In general terms, corporate reputation can be defined as the sum of the perceptions and assessments of all relevant stakeholders with regard to the performance, products, services, persons, organizations, etc. of a company and the respect for the company that arises from each of these factors," (Wiedmann & Buxel, 2005, p. 146).

How then can successful stakeholders create a backlash against their own interests? By the given definition, the reputation of a corporation should be an asset, so how can an asset damage the bottom line to a corporation? "Corporate reputation is increasingly regarded as a highly valued, intangible asset that is difficult to imitate and accordingly may provide a sustainable competitive advantage," (Reddiar, Kleyn, & Abratt, 2012, p. 29). It appears that corporate reputation is something to monitor and value.

How then, does a corporation get a reputation, good or bad? A "corporation's reputation is based mostly on non-rational, emotional aspects and/or incidental experience with one important evaluative aspect of the company," (Groenland, 2002, p. 308). A corporation's investors, employees, consumers, and even a corporation's competition, all converge to create a corporation's reputation. The difference between a good or bad reputation is: "what happens when the two broad aspects of reputation ratings come into conflict with strong, visionary management seen as leading a company to high and sustained financial success at the expense of customers, staff and communities. In these circumstances, at least in Australia, the effect is not a trade-off, but a backlash," (Porritt, 2005, p. 201).

Basu and Plazzo (2008) further develop the idea of all of these entities influencing the reputation of a corporation. They explore the idea of a corporation's social responsibility in bringing out the "*cognitive,* which implies thinking about the organization's relationships with its stakeholders and views about the broader world (i.e., the "common good" that goes beyond what's good for business), as well as the rationale for engaging in specific activities that might have an impact on key relationships," (page 124).

The reasoning for "seeking *cognitive* legitimacy, [where] a firm aligns its actions to be congruent with perceived societal expectations," (Basu & Palazzo, 2008, p. 126) appears to seek to increase its corporate reputation.

Past literature analyses of the construct of "corporate reputation" suggest that the definition has been obscured with measurement of its drivers; antecedents have been used regularly to measure the construct. This process has confounded our understanding of how corporations' reputations are formed and has made interpretation of both academic and practitioner research difficult (Ponzi, Fombrun, & Gardberg, 2011).

After extensive research on the subject of managing the integration and harmonization of the airspace for UAVs and manned systems, it appears clear that the U.S. government must develop policies, doctrines, and treaties that establish procedures and protocols for managing the uses and addressing the potential threats to national and international security posed by unmanned vehicles and robotics. A cooperative effort on the part of the FAA, the UAV community, the manned aircraft community, and law makers at all levels must be to manage and lead in non-traditional ways. The hard problems do not lend themselves to linear thinking. In addition, the U.S. government must share appropriate aspects of these policy documents to gain international consensus. Addressing both global and homeland security issues in the draft policies allows individual countries autonomy for their homeland security while creating the framework for the commercial industrial sector. Government agencies have vacillated on making a decision on which direction to choose and now they need the assistance of professional and commercial organizations to create the regulations that all parties can follow to flourish.

Unmanned vehicles and robotics pose an interesting policy and governance issue, one that does not fit the traditional policy realm since flexibility will be key to any implementation attempts. What traditional policy tends to miss is the human factor and how the policy will meet the human needs of the population it is intending to impact. Although originally designed for non-profit organizations, if John Carver's Policy Governance model is adapted to the UAV issue, it would allow social science to include the human needs into the development of hardware and software. In this adaptation, the board would be a government body. Carver's Policy Governance Model states:

"Ends: The board defines which human needs are to be met, for whom, and at what cost. Written from a long-term perspective, these mission-related policies embody most of the board's part of long-range planning…the prediction of outcomes is by means of the Ends policies (human needs). However, Policy Governance is considerably less deterministic than traditional strategic planning, where the prediction not only extends to the outcomes achieved, but even the strategies by which they will be achieved and the scheduling of those strategies," (as cited in Hough, 2002, p. 3).

The new, automated, non-physical world of cyber that controls unmanned vehicles and robotics, with its ability to be automated and programmed with predetermined responses, forces our thinking into new directions. Duke University professor Charles Dunlap was quoted in June 2012 saying:

"News reports that DARPA [Defense Advanced Research Projects Agency] is seeking proposals for methodologies that would automate cyber responses in predetermined scenarios is an almost inevitable development given the speed in which cyber-attacks can cause harm. The very idea of autonomous weapons systems of any kind, cyber or kinetic, is controversial on legal, ethical and even pragmatic warfighting grounds. Yet the development and deployment of such weaponry is sure to continue even as we sort out the law and policies to address it," (Wolverton, 2012, para 11).

The fact that UAVs in the future will become decision makers and not just navigators brings a new dimension to the process.

The standard government policy methodology may not work to bind and control this type of technology and its uses. The realism the world may face is that, with such a late start into this new policy realm, there may only be compromise left on the table as to how far humanity allows this to go. At the current rate of development, there may not be enough time left to implement policy and governance leaving only strategic negotiations to create limits on the lethal uses of the technology. In a 2012 *New York Times* article, Henning notes that, "without a new doctrine for the use of drones that is understandable to friends and foes, the United States risks achieving near-term tactical benefits in killing terrorists while incurring potentially significant longer-term cost to its alliance," (Henning, 2012, para 5).

If you send a leader to school to learn how to change a tire on a car and these leaders come back from training and only know how to make hamburgers both your money and your time have been wasted. This is precisely what the government has been doing in the cyber field. Leaders in the cyber field must be well-rounded and the technology is the easier part of the equation, what we deem as "the wetware interface" or the human is the tough part. Persuading users to not take actions that put the network in danger is a training and awareness issue.

Getting the security engineers to follow checklists and processes so systems are properly updated, patched and configured is a delicate dance of dealing with introverts who do not always take direction well and risk compromising the network. Learning to deal with lawyers, acquisition officials, stakeholders, relentless hackers and enemies of the state is a challenge best met with continuous leadership development and a heavy dose of technical skills. This type of training is specialized and the government does not appear to understand it, nor do they appear to have any desire to comprehend the science behind it. This is why one must "Think long and short term developmental implications when considering leadership education, training, and experience," (Hunt, 1996, p. 298).

CHAPTER SIX

Research Study-Managing the Integration and Harmonization of National Airspace for Unmanned and Manned Systems

> *Strategy is a process by which we can ensure the future and develop necessary steps to influence and achieve that future.*
>
> –Hans Mumm (Mumm, 2014)

INTRODUCTION

This study used the qualitative research method combined with grounded theory. Social science studies often utilize grounded theory. The process uses words and rich language to describe and analyze qualitative data. The qualitative data collected will tell the story that will provide an understanding of the posed research questions. Quantitative data uses numbers, graphs, and charts to tell a story about the collected data, however, the story is rooted in proving or disproving a hypothesis. Qualitative analysis using grounded theory allows themes to arise, thus, discovering deeper meaning from the data. A line of inquiry or any new theory can be the basis for additional studies. In the case of interviews, participants' views, thoughts, ideas and emotions reveal a deeper meaning than literature alone. Grounded theory allows the data to tell a story within the analysis; there is not a specific hypothesis that the investigator is attempting to prove. Instead, the investigator seeks to discover the meaning within the data. Corbin and Strauss (2008) said, "In qualitative research, the use of theoretical frameworks is not so clear," (page 39). The investigator is able to (a) work with the data, (b) look at it in different ways, and (c) compare and contrast meanings, themes and lines of inquiry far beyond what a set of numbers can describe in a quantitative research project.

Grounded theory uses qualitative data to answer a research question; the data collected moves the research project forward and determines the project's direction. Corbin and Strauss (2008) also state, "The purpose of the question is to lead the research into the data where the issues and problems important to the person, organization, groups and communities under investigation can be explored," (p. 25). The research questions describe the investigation's topic area, however, they are less restrictive in nature than a traditional hypothesis. The investigator writes research questions that focus on the social science aspects of individuals or members of a group under examination. Grounded theory is used in examining leadership and organizational change management and draws on data collected to "use the grounded theory regarding individual response to organizational change in the preparation and development of managers engaged in the implementation of change processes," (Egan, 2002, p. 292). Exploring meaning, drawing comparisons and developing understanding for this data are the goals. Instead of collecting to create a right or wrong argument, qualitative researchers seek to create a greater understanding of the world around us.

Researching in the social science arena requires the ability to gather data by observing, surveying, calculating, collecting and compiling large data sets from a population of interest. The researcher takes this information and places it against a given set of parameters, analyzing it not only for correct calculations, but also for utilizing human curiosity and integrating it with the gift of intellect to create knowledge from the data sets. This knowledge can confirm or deny the hypothesis or lead the researcher to additional questions and lines of query not originally discussed or envisioned by the researcher's hypothesis (Creswell, 2009).

Description of the Research Design

The research and discovery for this study consisted of UAV market research, including the private, commercial, and military market segments, a literature review and selected individual interviews. The approach allows for the widest range of data collection and data correlation to the grounded theory, which is not an entirely linear process in it of itself and, thus, lends itself well to this research.

The first data collection consisted of market research and a literature review. The individual interviews occurred during the second round of data collection. Coding the data from these interview sessions uncovered the emerging themes, concepts and theories in support of the original research questions. Integrating this coded data and analysis along with the market research and literature review created new knowledge and understanding in the leadership arena by using complexity theory in the area of managing the integration and harmonization of UAVs into the NAS.

Grounded Theory

Theory building is one of several advantages of using the grounded theory. The subject matter at hand has had little research completed and little theory built around it. This approach does not allow any single theoretical perspective to receive focus, allowing for a more complete and less biased research study. Grounded theory allows the investigator the flexibility to take the research in the direction of the data instead of allowing the research to dictate the data and the direction. Empirical observations, data and findings bring up additional questions and research directions and themes that the original research proposal may not have considered. This allows the examination of the research questions to "establish emerging impressions from the evidence, conceptualizing the data and then analyzes emerging relationships between concepts," (Egan, 2002, p. 278). Grounded theory is outlined in the following steps: "(a) initiating research (b) data selection (c) initiation and ongoing data collection (d) data analysis (e) concluding the research" (Egan, 2002, p. 280).

Grounded theory is a qualitative analysis framework. It is a way of theorizing without an overabundant reliance on narrow theories or themes that may limit substantive discovery or the investigator's intuitive research processes. Grounded theory provides a model from which to think and to work out inquisitive thought, to analyze the data and to draw meaning from the data without preconceived notions on what the data should be telling the investigator. There is a continuous interplay between analysis and data, without the need to prove or disprove a hypothesis.

Many authors who research organizations, organizational change, change management, and leadership themes successfully employ the grounded theory approach. One of the keys to success in this vein occurs when the "emphasis is placed on grounded theory's ability to facilitate understanding and to identify desirable improvements in work contexts" (Martin & Turner, 1986, p. 141). The validity and acceptance of grounded theory combined with other theories and existing research strengthens the theory building and is "the essence of this reversal from the typical deductive-to-inductive approach to research…to avoid exploring the phenomenon on the predisposition in existing literature," (Egan, 2002, p. 279). Decisions regarding the emergence of categories and themes are determined as data is collected. This can alter the data collection strategies to explore one phenomenon more in-depth than another while allowing for theory building to continue. This is difficult for some researchers to grasp because the flexibility of grounded theory, in some ways, is opposite to traditional approaches. The traditional approach can be viewed as an impediment to modification of the collection process in mid-stream, which can also limit the insight gained throughout the research process. Grounded theory allows for ongoing collection adjustments—this is accepted and expected throughout the research; it does not skew the results, it enhances them.

Grounded theory research is considered complete "when the research has observed a point of data saturation and a sufficient theory has emerged from the data. Data saturation is evident when data collection no longer contributes to elaboration of the phenomenon being investigated,"

(Egan, 2002, p. 286). Upon saturation level, no new research is collected. The singular focus is on the construction of theory through data coding and the documentation of the analysis and future research themes to further develop the topic under investigation. The criteria for evaluating grounded theory is not conventional and will lean more on one's ability to evaluate the analytical logic, processes, and logic flows used by the researcher than a standard yard stick of a perceived right or wrong answer. Analytical methodologies are used at times to support logic within the research; however, they are not required in the strictest sense to validate the theoretical arguments being presented in the findings.

COMPLEXITY THEORY

In an ever-evolving world that appears to be more complex than ever, the world must keep in mind that "fundamental changes in sciences offer new perspectives for the management of complexity. Increased complexity in society, economics, and technology requires a new and suitable organization and management," (Saynisch, 2010, p. 21).

Complexity theory began in the 1980s, significantly through the work of the Santa Fe Institute. "In some sense, the *ancien régime* of chaos theory has given way to the study of complexity as 'life at the edge of chaos'... In complexity theory, a system can be described as a collection of interacting parts, which together function as a whole.... This interaction is so intricate that it cannot be predicted by linear equations; there are so many variables involved that the behavior of the system can only be understood as an "emerging consequence" of the sum of the constituent elements," (Morrison, 2002, p. 13).

UAV integration exhibits the earmarks of a complex problem: there are twelve primary stakeholders and twenty key issues that are fundamental to the leadership, management, and technical solution. In addition, the level of satisfaction is often non-linear for each combination of stakeholder and issue.

Creating a complexity leadership foundation begins with actionable vision. Actionable is the key word. The vision should guide every decision, large or small, made during the process. When in doubt, refer back to the vision statement for guidance. One cannot stress enough the level of importance of the vision and the accompanying philosophies. One must drill down to the core for these items and operate from the corner of success. This investigator recommends the following vision: create the simplest path possible for the UAV community to integrate fully into the National Airspace System.

Next, create a set of philosophies to accompany the vision. The number of governing philosophies to create is based on the correct number that it takes to guide the vast majority of key decisions. Typically, these philosophies already will have the fundamental decision imbedded in them. To clarify, they must be concise, easy to remember and follow, and only as many as necessary to guide the majority of decisions.

The leadership must instill the vision and philosophies into the solution's participants. For the stakeholders that are not participants in the process, it should give them confidence that the challenge is being attacked in the best manner possible. In this case, the investigator's recommended set of philosophies and the reasons are discussed throughout the remainder of the chapter.

UNSAFE FLIGHTS?

Flying is not inherently safe. The FAA's core responsibility is to manage the risk and the air traffic in a manner that provides a high degree of satisfaction to all users of the NAS. The two key words in this philosophy are *significant* and *human*. Adding any flying vehicle to the current airspace increases risk; adding one that is unaware of its surroundings adds more risk. This risk can be managed and be reasonable. Currently, the FAA experiences one fatal accident in roughly 100,000 flight hours for general aviation aircraft and about one in one million flight hours for commercial jet aircraft. UAVs currently lose one hull in roughly 10,000 hours, depending on the size and maturity of the UAV. Because only ground personnel (groundlings) have any risk of injury from a UAV, UAVs should not make an impact on the overall national fatality numbers. The current probability of a groundling fatality is about one in 100 million (Thompson, Rabouw, & Cooke, 2001). UAVs can achieve the one in 100 million standards by flying over the 85% of the country that does not include large population density.

The second word, "human," is a key discriminator. The vast majority of the regulations and policies the FAA has generated in the past, work to protect those on board. UAVs currently carry no one; therefore, they do not need regulation to protect anyone onboard. FAA regulations and policies do not always match the conditions of UAVs; UAVs cannot simply adopt them. The risk to humans on the ground is miniscule in rural areas and low in urban areas. The physical space that humans take up, even in urban areas, is relatively small in relation to the size of the available UAV flight operations areas. The risk to other aircraft that do have humans on board is a management and technology challenge. Except for airways and airport traffic areas, the airspace is vast and relatively uncongested.

EXPERIMENTATION IS THE ONLY PATH TO GROWTH

The marketplace for UAVs is demanding and expanding rapidly. Many new designs must appear to fill the multitude of military, commercial, and government missions. To meet the demanding customer requirements, the UAVs will in many cases require a creative design. Unlike manned aircraft, UAVs undergo continuous modification. This means that there will be a long-term demand for experimental flight operations in the UAV's life cycle. Even though cost is a key driver throughout the UAV life cycle, it is most important during the early stages.

UAV airspace experimentation is critical to the pace of integration into the NAS. Only by actually flying UAVs on a regular basis in the NAS will we really know what is necessary, what is superfluous, and what boundaries match between the individual UAV and the NAS. Early experimental operations in Classes E and G airspace offer an opportunity to move quickly along the learning curve.

Outcome

In nature and humans, we see macro behaviors. What lays behind those macro behaviors are all of the unseen micro decisions that lead to those behaviors. Guided by micro decisions are the overall vision or goal and the set of philosophies or rules. These can be as simple as stay to the right of the center line on the road. As the road twists and turns, the micro decision based on that rule repeatedly happens. Combined with the other appropriate rules, the macro behavior of driving down the road occurs. This is the emergent behavior. When the stakeholders come together to solve an issue, they will be making many micro decisions based on the vision and philosophies that lead to macro solutions. Multiple stakeholder-issue groups would operate in parallel and provide interim results to the other groups. A set of procedures that effectively covers the initial integration of UAVs into the NAS should emerge. Then the normal process of evolutionary rulemaking can begin to fine-tune the procedures based on experience.

Target Population

The target population for this study was subject matter experts (SMEs) from the aviation industry. This included (a) members of the UAV community, (b) manned aircraft pilots, (c) FAA policy officials, (d) UAV manufacturers, and (e) Homeland Security Aviation Operations. The researcher used the same interview questions to discuss UAVs with four people from each of the five organizations. The common threads that tied these five groups together included the aviation industry, homeland security issues, airworthiness, and flight safety. By using these five industry groups, the investigator extrapolated the thoughts, feelings, and opinions within the different groups on the use of a complexity theory leadership style to facilitate the integration and harmonization of UAVs into the NAS.

The five organizations agreed to allow four noted SME interviews each for this study: The AUVSI, U.S. Airline Pilot Association (USAPA), UAV manufacturers, the FAA, and DHS.

DATA COLLECTION PROCEDURES

Data triangulation began with the first data collection method: market research. Triangulation continued through a literature review and follow-up with data collected through one-on-one interviews. The market research included all sectors of the aviation industry, the military and civilian uses of UAVs, the historical change agents in the aviation industry and the governmental and political forces on the overall aviation industry. This research brought forth the steady idea from the aviation industry as a whole that progress could, and should, be made in the integration of UAVs into the NAS; however, it appears that the political and regulatory issues are impeding this progress. Numerous academic and industry articles agree that "commercial interest for unmanned aircraft systems (UASs) has seen a steady increase over the last decade; nevertheless, UAS operations have remained almost exclusively military. This is mainly due to the lack of a regulatory framework," (Dalamagkidis, Valavanis, & Piegl, 2008, p. 503).

The literature review, methodically created, walked the reader through dozens of journals, case studies and articles in the current literature collection on the subject. The review is broken into sections concerning the issues, technology, current status, and a possible solution to the challenge of adapting a complexity style leadership model to the problem. The last part of the literature review examined corporate reputation management and branding. The public relations aspect of change management cannot be understated. The FAA and the aviation industry must be in lock step for the legislators and citizens to believe in the solution and the safety aspects of the framework.

Individual interviews will occur during the second round of data collection. Coding the data from these interview sessions allowed for in-depth data analysis. Through data analysis, the investigator will seek to understand emerging themes, concepts and theories in support of the original research questions. In the final step, the investigator will analyze and synthesize this coded data with the market research and literature review, thereby creating new knowledge and understanding in the area of complexity theory leadership and its application to the integration and harmonization of UAV into the NAS.

The interviews took place at the offices of the five organizations located in the northern Virginia and Washington DC area. The participants signed an informed consent form. The participants also completed a demographic information sheet. The investigator read aloud the opening paragraph of the research questions, provided a short tabletop briefing of the key concepts (Appendix B), and the participants answered the research questions in the form of a questionnaire (Appendix C).

The participants selected are SMEs in the aviation field active stakeholders in the integration of UAVs into the NAS. This allowed for a range of samples from the five organizations and their noted experts, as they may have a stake in the outcome of this study and the successful integration of UAV into the NAS. This gave the investigator an indication whether or not the SMEs in these five organizations will embrace the leadership direction change that is proposed. The SMEs and their organizations have unique perspectives concerning how they see the traditional role of policy and change management leadership, particularly from view of the aviation industry. These sample groups also tend to be well-versed and well-read when it comes to the current state and future outlook of the aviation market place. They also tend to know why past initiatives have failed and are advocates for a developing a working solution to the problem of integrating UAVs into the NAS.

The interview questions used for this qualitative study were:

1. How might the FAA employ a complexity style of change management to integrate UAVs into the NAS?

2. How could the employment of a complexity style of change management expedite the integration of UAVs into the NAS?

3. What critical leadership issues impede the movement of UAVs into the NAS?

4. Based on the study's explanation of integrating UAVs into the NAS using a complexity style of leadership, would you favor this normative change if it could accelerate the process of integrating UAVs into the NAS? (Why or Why not?)

5. How do you think the complexity style of leadership could help your stakeholder group?

6. What are your thoughts on using a complexity leadership model that would allow the UAV stakeholder community to create the rules that govern UAVs in the NAS and the FAA approving them?

Reflecting on the interview itself, the investigator needed to be cognizant of his own actions during these interviews. The investigator did not want any of his own actions or interview style to influence the participants' answers or behaviors. Rubin (2012) discusses slant probes which "help you determine the lenses through which people see and interpret their worlds" (page 147). The investigator has had single engine land pilot license for twenty-one years, with helicopter time starting in 1997. The investigator began his journey in the UAV industry in 1999. The investigator recognized the possibility for biases due to these experiences. This investigator recognized this bias and minimized it by mixing organizations interviewed, using unbiased coders, and soliciting and receiving reviews by Colorado Technical University (CTU) professors.

Data Analysis

The research and discovery for this study consisted of separate interviews with four SMEs from five selected organizations, using the research questions and questionnaire as a guide. The approach allowed for the widest range of data collection and data correlation using a one-on-one interview process to guide the study and grounded theory to document the findings.

Manual coding is appropriate; the data collection is small enough that it is easy to decipher. An example is provided below of manual coding during a single in-person data collection effort and a review of previous studies on the subject. It is clear that coding software for larger data sets would allow the investigator to manipulate and ponder the data more easily. Coding software allows for data manipulation and re-coding through multiple lenses and coding schemes to bring out the stories that the data can tell. The software tends to be complicated to learn, use and to save the final data set.

The coding below is an example of a study to look to see if an individual's demographics could influence the source and opinions on corporate reputation value. In addition to exploring any bias, the interviewed subjects in this example offered insight into the possible correlation to demographics and political party affiliation. The use of this example is only to illustrate the investigator's knowledge concerning the ideas and concepts surrounding the use of theme-based coding that is typical while using grounded theory.

Participants Demographic

The investigator and twenty participants took part in this study. Five organizations, (a) the AUVSI, (b) USAPA, (c) the FAA, (d) selected UAV manufactures, and (e) DHS, allowed SME interviews for this study.

BENEFITS TO PARTICIPANTS

There may or may not be direct benefits to the participants in this study; however, it is hoped that the study illustrates the participants' thoughts and opinions on how they perceive using a new leadership style for change management. This new leadership system is an adaptation of the complexity theory applied to managing the integration and harmonization of UAVs into the NAS. It explores how this normative change may affect the participant's opinions of the current leadership approach. The data collected also may also offer a correlation between the participants' perceptions and their willingness to work with a new type of leadership style. This could allow them to collaborate and coordinate more throughout the aviation industry. This could offer insight into the willingness of current and prospective aviation SMEs to work with a new leadership style that offers non-traditional ways of creating policies and governance. The investigator envisions reporting the study data to the academic community, the aviation industry, military briefings, seminars and symposia. The results of the study should provide a deeper understanding of complexity theory and how it can be adapted to create new leadership styles allowing for new complex solutions in a more rapid fashion and with greater human understanding.

PROTECTION OF DATA SOURCES

All information gathered in this study were kept completely confidential. No reference was made in written or oral materials that might link individuals or participants to this study. All data and discovery for this research project was coded and analyzed for use in the final research study was published and briefed to the academic and business communities. All demographic information was destroyed at the conclusion of the study.

THREATS TO EXTERNAL VALIDITY

External validity refers to the extent to which the results of a study are generalizable to other situations and to other people and populations. External validity asks, can the results of the study be generalized beyond this study, and in this case they can be due to a narrow range of questions generalized to a small specialized population in the aviation industry, verses the overall US population.

In qualitative research, this concept is the ability for the researcher to transfer to many different yet similar situations with similar parameters, populations and characteristics. In this case the confidence placed in the external validity of the study is very high as the study results refers to leadership and unique leadership paradigms that can offer new ways of designing leadership frameworks for several different population sectors.

The instrument used to collect the third triangle of data for the study is the one-on-one interview. This instrument is a tried and true instrument for collecting qualitative data from participants. The participants received no compensation for their time or the answers they provided. The investigator read the same opening paragraph to each participant to prepare participants for the interview questions. The identical research questions were administered to the participants in the same order and same number of questions.

THREAT TO INTERNAL VALIDITY

The internal validity of a study is really asking was the research done correctly. By limiting the data collection time to fewer than forty-five days, the integrity of the internal validity of this study was maintained and ensured. This limited the likelihood of events overtaking the results of this study or any of the identified participants from passing away before they were interviewed.

Events outside of the study such as lethal drone attacks overseas, the Whitehouse drone incident and Fourth Amendment Rights rallies could affect participants' responses to the research questions and every effort was made to track news stories during the 45-day collection timeframe.

No documented historical events, rallies or legislation appeared in the news media during this 45 days period. The selected participants are all SMEs in the aviation field. The SMEs work in different locations surrounding the metropolitan Washington DC area. Participants are employed by different organizations; the opportunity for collusion or one participant calling another to discuss the interview questions ahead of time was considered minimal.

Investigator bias was controlled by the use of independent triangulation coding schemes ensured the reliability of the results. The investigator and two independent coders with master's degrees and knowledge of the UAV industry coded the data. The coders live in geographically separate areas. Encrypting the data files and the results while in transit ensured the safety of the data files.

CHAPTER SEVEN

"All human behavior has a reason. All behavior is solving a problem."

Michael Crichton, Disclosure (Crichton, 2014, p. 3)

| DATA GATHERED AND FINDINGS REPORTED

This section of the document details the data collected, the participant demographics and the interview findings with unexpected findings highlighted by the investigator. This qualitative case study research gathered data through interviews. The investigator designed the interviews to collect information on the topic of adapting a complexity model of leadership and organizational change management to the issue of integrating and harmonizing UAVs into the NAS.

The research utilized grounded theory which allows data that "is discovered empirically, through induction, not deduction," (Egan, 2002, p. 277). The study used inductive reasoning principles to identify leadership issues that may contribute to the difficulty integrating and harmonizing unmanned and manned vehicles into the NAS. This study examined the convergence of these leadership challenges to answer the research questions: (a) How might the FAA employ a complexity style of change management to integrate UAVs into the NAS? (b) Could the employment of a complexity style of change management expedite the integration of UAVs into the NAS? (c) What are the critical leadership issues impeding the movement of UAVs into the NAS?

Although the UAS industry is unique and rapidly evolving, the leadership and organizational challenges are not; therefore, a case study approach is appropriate for a scholarly inquiry of this social phenomenon.

This research used interviews to collect data. The average time associated with each interview was eight-to-ten hours. This included the time to (a) source the subject matter expert, (b) make the initial contact and obtain consent for the interview, (c) schedule the interview, (d) discuss the research, (e) conduct the interview, and (f) the investigator's travel time. The total time for these investigative interviews was just over 200 hours over approximately five weeks. Following each interview, the investigator sent a courtesy correspondence to thank the participants for his involvement. All twenty interviews were audio-recorded by the investigator. Two separate individuals reviewed the resulting transcripts for quality control. After the quality control inspection, two coders received the final transcript and audio file to ensure that all coding resulted from the same information. The investigator completed the demographics analysis and performed a third set of coding. The investigator then compiled the results of the coding and analyzed it for themes, noting any unexpected results. Coding and analysis took an average of eight-to-ten hours per interview. This time excluded any follow-ups or additional information gathered from any unique data discovered during the interview session.

Most of the participants had a few questions about the consent form and demographics form. Participants wanted to know how the randomly selected participant number was going to maintain their anonymity. The interviewer reviewed the methodology and provided a response that satisfied the participants.

PARTICIPANT DEMOGRAPHICS

For this study, the investigator sought subject matter experts in three areas: aviation, UAVs, and the government policies that govern the use of UAVs in the NAS. The researcher sought four participants from each of the following five organizations: (a) the AUVSI, (b) USAPA, (c) UAV manufacturers, (d) the FAA, and (e) DHS. The FAA provided two participants and DHS provided four. Four SMEs, either as current or former FAA contractors, augmented the six federal employees. These SMEs have experience writing recommendations for the Aviation Rules Committee (ARC) or FAA policies for general aviation.

All twenty participants were male, however, this was not unexpected as the aviation industry is male-dominated. A 2012 study discussed many reasons and implications of this gender dominance (Germain, Herzog, & Hamilton, 2012).

As shown in Figure 14, the participants' predominant age was 47 years old or older with fifteen participants in this age range. Three participants were in the 37-46 age range, two in the 25-36 range and one in the 18-24 range. The investigator also expected this result. As the aviation industry continues to grow, change and mature, many of the SMEs for this field are at the higher age ranges; however, the UAV and remotely piloted industry is beginning to get younger people involved. The two participants in the 18-36 age range noted that their involvement started in grade school as programmers for the robotics aspect of this industry.

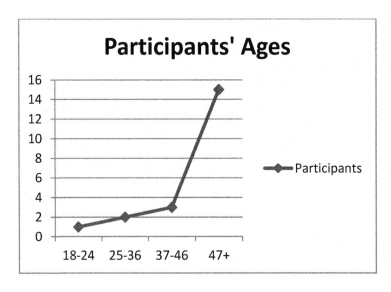

Figure 14 - Participants' Ages

Figure 15 provides the participants' employer demographics. The employer breakdown is as expected: (a) six government employees, (b) four government contractors, (c) eight private company employees, (d) one tenured university staff member, and (e) one retired aviation employee who now works as an industry consultant. Since UAVs are an emerging industry, the investigator finds it interesting that the SMEs are in the private sector and not in the government or academia. The technology is being developed and refined in the private sector.

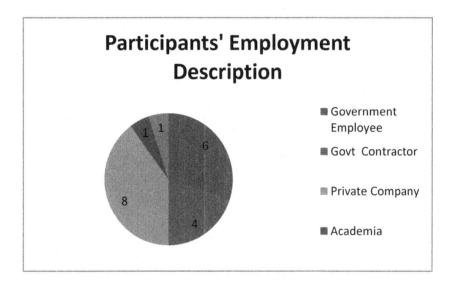

Figure 15 - Participants' Employment Descriptions

All of the participants were U.S. citizens and they all worked full time in the industry except for one participant who worked full time in the industry and had a second job outside of the aviation industry.

Figure 16 provides a summary of the participants' education level. Of the participants, two participants completed high school, nine participants have undergraduate degrees, seven have graduate degrees, and two have doctorate degrees.

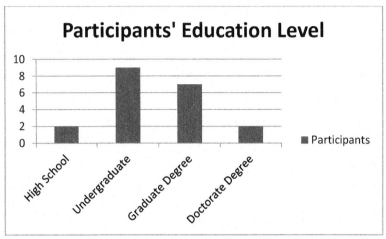

Figure 16 - Participants' Education Level

The participants had a wide range of experience in the industry. The newest member had two years of experience (with an additional four years of experience in control theory) and the most senior participants had over thirty-seven years of experience. The average level of experience was seventeen years.

Two participants indicated that they held stock in the aviation industry and sixteen participants did not hold industry stock. The two remaining participants were unsure, noting that their 401K retirement accounts might hold these stocks; however, they did not have immediate influence in the purchase or sale of the stock.

The participants split evenly with ten having experience writing government policy and ten that had not written government policy.

Since all of the participants have the common thread of aviation, these demographics offer potential insight into their answers. In addition, what may appear to be 20 participants pulling in the same direction may not be true; their unique experiences, values, thoughts, ideas and motivations vary. The participants have different backgrounds, years of experience, and financial motivations. The one thread that holds them all together is that they are all working through the issues of integrating UAVs into the NAS.

PRESENTATION OF THE DATA

Sixteen of the twenty interviews (80%) were in-person interviews and the other four were phone interviews. At the beginning of the interview, the investigator provided time for the participant to read and complete the consent form and the demographics form. In lieu of an opening statement, the investigator provided a uniform tabletop briefing that described the research to the participants. This approach provided information to the participants in the same format and sequence, reducing any research bias, while informing the participants about the research. A tabletop briefing allowed for a discussion between the investigator and the participant that may not have occurred had the investigator simply read a statement directly to the participant. Appendix B contains the tabletop briefing.

The final part of the interview allowed the participant to respond to the research questions. The research questions allowed the participants to explore the idea of adapting a complexity style of leadership to the organizational and leadership challenges associated with integrating and harmonizing UAVs into the NAS.

All of the participants agreed that integrating UAVs into the NAS is a complex issue. In-depth consideration and study must take place to develop a leadership model for this complex environment. How complex is this challenge? In the course of one interview, the participant provided the investigator a "mind map," created by the MITRE Corporation. As shown in Figure 17, this mind map offers insight into the complexity of the UAS community interactions by graphically illustrating the interactions between stakeholders and issues. Strong leadership and organizational skills must be in order to take command of this complex issue. Some stakeholders and issues interact with each other while other stakeholders and issues do not directly interact, but they are all part of the larger issue under investigation. This graphic, used with permission from the MITRE Corporation, provides a glimpse into the complexity that the FAA experiences in order to integrate UAVs into the NAS.

The investigator and two independent parties, with master's degrees and several years of leadership and research knowledge, coded the collected interview results. The use of two independent coders reaffirms the reliability of the results and reduces the possibility of any investigator results bias. All three sets of coded results showed strong similarity providing evidence of neutral, unbiased results. Minor deviations can be attributed to individual coders' interpretations and not to any skewing of the data; the same major themes were evident in each coder's results. In addition to their responses to the prepared questions, the interview participants provided valuable insights and meaningful contextual information. These insights reveal deeper meaning and emotions on the subject; coding captured this contextual information.

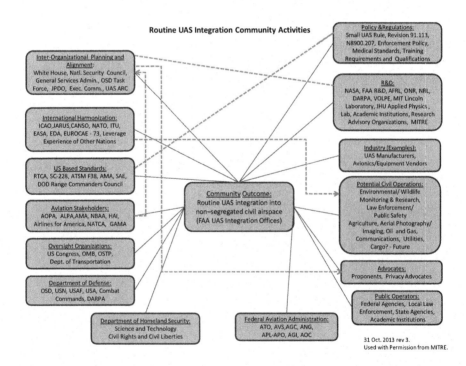

Figure 17 - UAS Community Interactions Mind Map

The MITRE Corporation prepared this mind map in an effort to capture key stakeholders involved with the routine integration of UAS into non-segregated civil airspace. It represents an opinion, not official organizational structures or characterizations. 31 October 2013 rev 3. (C) 2013. The MITRE Corporation. All Rights Reserved.

The investigator created and labeled twenty-one relevant categories to capture potential themes before coding commenced. The categories define research themes (leadership and organizational change management) that map back to the three main research questions in order to capture the intensity of those themes and other themes that emerged during the interview process.

The coders used the audio files and the available transcripts from Cogi—an audio transcription service. The Cogi process for transcribing uploaded audio files was an extremely slow compared process for the interviews conducted over the phone that used the Cogi linking transcribing service.

The investigator provided the two coders with the audio recording, interview transcripts and notes. The coders independently verified the quality of the transcripts with the recordings and the investigator's interview notes. The coded data collection effort utilized a spreadsheet containing the 21 categories correlated to the 20 participants' responses. The coders and investigator met on several occasions to review material. Using three separate sets of coded data allowed the investigator an opportunity to discover any coding bias. The coding from the independent coders was similar to the investigator's coded data set, although not identical. The same theme trends were evident in all three of the coded data sets, with two exceptions. The first exception was whether the participant believes that the public perception of UAVs may slow the pace toward integration. This discrepancy is most likely due to outside media bias influencing some of the coders. This outside influence is not a controllable factor due to the amount of exposure UAVs have had in the media recently, especially relating to fourth amendment issues. Political fights over controversial legislation such as the *Patriot Act, The Foreign Surveillance Act (FISA) and Intelligence Reform and Terrorism Act* created the sense that it was politics as usual in Washington. The second exception relates to the relative difficulty in integrating small UAVs compared to large UAVs. This theme often emerged in the overall context of the answers and implied in discussions, however, it was not as a direct statement. One of the independent coders was less familiar with the integration challenges and did not always identify this contextual relationship. These two exceptions may account for the slight deviations in the findings. The three coders worked independently throughout the coding process.

Although all three coders produced similar results, there were a few differences. The investigator decided that combining the three coders' results would best way capture the data. Table 5 shows these composite results. The maximum theme intensity of twenty participants per coder became sixty upon combining the coded data between the three coders. Appendix D shows the integrated coding results.

Table 5 – Interview Intensity

Description	Intensity
Participant believes current leadership method is the cause for UAV integration process proceeding too slowly	45
Participant believes the UAV integrations process is proceeding fast enough or too fast	11
Participant believes the UAV integration process is too complex for the usual linear organizational and leadership problem solving methodology	48
Participant believes the UAV integration process is simple and straightforward	1
Participant believes that the use of complexity leadership theory could accelerate the process.	46
Participant believes that the use of complexity leadership theory would not help the process.	13
Participant believes the problem is primarily a leadership issue.	31

Description	Intensity
Participant believes the problem is primarily a technology issue.	2
Participant believes the problem is both management and technology related.	22
Participant believes his stakeholder group would embrace the use of complexity leadership and management theory to facilitate the process.	51
Participant believes his stakeholder group would not embrace the use of complexity leadership and management theory to facilitate the process.	6
Participant believes the current set of regulations for UAVs to fly in the NAS is unacceptable.	40
Participant believes his stakeholder group is happy with the current state of affairs.	12
Participant believes there is a significant pent up **commercial** UAV demand for operations in the NAS.	45
Participant believes there is a significant pent up **military** UAV demand for operations in the NAS.	25
Participant believes there is little or no demand for UAV operations in the NAS.	0
Participant believes the small UAVs will be the most difficult to integrate.	25
Participant believes the large UAVs will be the most difficult to integrate.	4
Participant believes the FAA could significantly harm the UAV business with overregulation.	25
Participant believes public perception of UAVs may slow the pace toward integration.	27
Outside group execution and submission to FAA support.	57

Interview Findings

The investigator analyzed the results of the interviews and identified both emergent themes and significant insights related to the leadership issues surrounding the integration of UAVs into the NAS. Table 6 provides this information in two parts: the emergent themes from the coding and significant insights from the participants.

Table 6 – Emergent Themes

Finding Number	Emergent Themes	Comments
1	Participant believes current leadership method is the cause for UAV integration process proceeding too slowly.	The current leadership method was designed for slow and incremental changes, not entirely new paradigms and accelerated schedules.
2	Participant believes the UAV integration process is too complex for the usual linear organizational and leadership problem solving methodology.	Multiple interviewees added knowledge of additional complexities that made the problem even more complex.
3	Participant believes that the use of complexity leadership theory could accelerate the process.	Most participants received this well. They felt the process was more inclusive and less rigid. They felt the structure lent itself to a much faster process.
4	Participant believes the problem is primarily a leadership issue.	Finding numbers 4 and 5 were nearly equal in the intensity of response. Those responding with 4 believed that if the leadership problems were resolved then the technology would resolve itself. Those responding with 5 also believed that key technology items that must be decided so the UAV community can move forward.
5	Participant believes the problem is both management and technology related.	
6	Participant believes his stakeholder group would embrace the use of complexity leadership and management theory to facilitate the process.	The participants generally believed that the enthusiasm for the complexity leadership model would be greater in their stakeholder group than in the FAA stakeholder group.
7	Participant believes there is a significant pent up commercial UAV demand for operations in the NAS.	Several of the participants expressed frustration with the lack of appropriate rules that would allow commercial operations in the NAS.
8	Participant believes there is a significant pent up military UAV demand for operations in the NAS.	The military demand did not seem to weigh much on the participants' minds, other than the relative power of their voice in the process.

Finding Number	Emergent Themes	Comments
9	Participant believes the small UAVs will be the most difficult to integrate.	Overwhelmingly, participants believed that the smaller UAVs would be harder to integrate. There were a variety of reasons, but the theme of a simplistic user (limited aerospace knowledge and limited UAV system capabilities) being forced into a regulatory world designed for large UAVs or even manned aircraft was prevalent. This was considered unacceptable.
10	Participant believes the FAA could significantly harm the UAV business with overregulation.	This was a prevalent fear based on recent FAA actions and trial balloon regulations.
11	Participant believes public perception of UAVs may slow the pace toward integration.	The coding of this theme may have been impacted by outside media influencing the coder.
12	Outside group execution and submission to FAA support.	This varied from modest support to very strong support, but almost universally, it was supported. The FAA understands its personnel and funding limitations and have extended their hand to several outside groups to help create the suggested path and fill a giant data gap.
13	The FAA team responsible for the integration have very few members.	The term "team" is used loosely as the members are not in the same organization.
14	The FAA outsources much of the work to outside organizations and one or more chartered committees.	FAA has outsourced work to two different ARCs, an executive committee (EXCOM), an FFRDC (MITRE), and multiple UAS test sites.
15	The federal rulemaking process that the FAA must follow takes a minimum of 5 years to complete for even simple rules.	The investigator quickly recognized this as the number one impediment to publishing timely UAS regulations and the degree to which the FAA's embrace of a complexity approach could accelerate the process. This problem is systemic within all government rulemaking organizations.

Finding Number	Emergent Themes	Comments
16	The small UAV companies (builders and users) that create the majority of the community felt left out of the process. They generally feel they are not being heard.	The very nature of the ARC process limits the number of members. There was little to no voice from the membership supporting the small UAV companies. Many of the small UAV companies have their whole business riding on the outcome of the FAA rulemaking process.
17	The FAA has very little data upon which to make decisions. This is one of the purposes of the six new UAV centers of excellence.	The data required to make the FAA's usual safety assessments will take many years to gather.
18	Not all UAVs are created equally. The rules need to delineate between levels of UAVs.	The current FAA plan lumps all UAVs 55 pounds and under into the same category. UAVs under 10 pounds, however, are vastly different from other 'small' UAVs in terms of capabilities and hazard to people and property. As costs have decreased, these very lightweight UAVs have proliferated significantly.
19	The UAV community believes the FAA is looking at all risk and no gain for the FAA.	The FAA has little or nothing to gain by integrating UAVs into the NAS. They have the risk of a negative safety impact on their current operations. The UAV community has both gain and risk in the rulemaking process and continued operations.
20	The judge in the Pirker ruled that the FAA has no oversight authority for UAVs (Levin, 2014).	The FAA is appealing the decision.
21	Congress is part of the leadership problem.	Congress needs to play a bigger role beyond just telling the FAA to get it done.

As shown in Table 5, the participant interviews coding revealed six prominent themes. The six themes are:

» Participants believed current leadership method is the cause for UAV integration process proceeding too slowly.

» Participants believed the UAV integration process is too complex for the usual linear organizational and leadership problem solving methodology.

» Participants believed that the use of complexity leadership theory could accelerate the process.

» Participants believed their stakeholder group would embrace the use of complexity leadership and management theory to facilitate the process.

» Participants believed there is a significant pent up commercial UAV demand for operations in the NAS.

» Participants believed that an outside group could create and execute rules through a concurrence and submission to FAA.

Articulating leadership themes from the data offers the ability to review the data from multiple lenses along with offering some ideas for future research. Table 7 delineates several leadership attributes that emerged from the data. Several participants considered the complexity model as a more effective leadership model for these attributes.

Table 7 – Leadership Attributes

» Trust, Responsibility	» Respect
» Accountability	» Conflict
» Change Management	» Conflict Management
» Empowerment	» Persuasion
» Innovation	» Clarity
» Measured Progress	» Integrity
» Application in Organization Group Dynamics	» Shared Vision and Actions
» Focus	» Collaboration
» Passion	» Self-Awareness
	» Leadership Transition

Leadership without authority is tenuous at best and this appears to be an issue at the FAA. Tasking the FAA to resolve the issue of how to integrate UAVs into the NAS is well within Congressional jurisdiction; however, the FAA does not have all of the necessary authorities to create the solution. The FAA is only part of the process, yet they are taking the brunt of the criticism.

Unexpected Findings from the Interviews

The interview process yielded a number of unexpected findings. The following unexpected findings are critical:

» The FAA appears focused on the technical solution; the UAV community appears focused on the leadership problems. The investigator and the coders discussed this and agreed that this was unexpected. During the initial research phase of this study, the investigator reasoned that the FAA would be more focused on the leadership solution.

» Only one interview participant's UAV operating organization was receiving next-day COA approvals for their UAVs to fly in the NAS. Every other requesting operator was part of the long FAA COA approval backlog. This illustrates that while the FAA struggles to create the rules, some groups appear relatively unscathed in the extremely long rulemaking process.

» The FAA, stymied with the federal rulemaking process, prevents the development of any timely rules for integrating UAVs into the NAS. One participant offered that only Congress could provide a solution to this extended timeline challenge. The investigator took this one step further and called several offices on Capitol Hill that have the ability to affect this process. The offices were adamant that the five-year rulemaking process must be followed. All offices agreed with the investigator, however, that if Congress wanted to, Congress could offer a waiver or an abbreviated process to allow UAVs into the NAS.

» The interview question concerning how the FAA could employ the complexity leadership model appeared to make several of the participants nervous. In delving into this topic, the participants admitted that this was often due to the belief that even though the FAA might embrace the concept, their bureaucracy and long-established processes might thwart the effort. Some participants, however, believed that the FAA could expand their ARC process to multiple simultaneous ARCs to achieve the intent of the complexity model and stay within the FAA's comfort zone.

» The Pirker court decision (Levin, 2014) that the FAA has no authority to regulate UAVs has the potential to change the entire process. The FAA is appealing this decision and is operating under the assumption that they control the airspace from the ground up, regardless of the type of aircraft.

» Ultralight aircraft (under 254 lbs.) operate in a self-regulated community with little FAA oversight.

  – The FAA has chosen not to promulgate Federal regulations regarding pilot certification, vehicle certification, and vehicle registration, preferring that the ultralight community assume the initiative for the development of these important safety programs. The ultralight community is expected to take positive action to develop these programs in a timely manner and gain FAA approval for their implementation (Connolly, 2014, para 3).

» Radio Controlled (RC) aircraft operate under a voluntary set of rules based on an FAA advisory circular. "This advisory circular outlines, and encourages voluntary compliance with, safety standards for model aircraft operators," (*Model Aircraft Operating Standards*, 1981, p. 1).

ADDITIONAL DATA COLLECTION OUTSIDE OF THE INTERVIEWS

As allowed by grounded theory, the data gathered in the interviews pointed out several additional data sources that would enhance the research. Several of the participants offered additional reports, presentations and seminars that allowed the investigator to develop a deeper understanding of the entire issue surrounding the organizational and leadership challenges of integrating UAVs into the NAS.

For example, after one interview, the participant introduced the investigator to the Drone User Group. This group is dedicated to the commercial use of drones for the benefit of all societies. It boasts a network of over four thousand members across North America, Australia, Asia and Europe. The investigator attended a Washington DC Drone User Group meeting where the Board for Conservation presented a governance framework describing how the group will use drones to engage in conservation activities in the Maryland, DC and Virginia areas. Endorsed by the local government, this activity assists in the creation of digital maps that will aid in vegetation and animal conservation in local parks and recreation areas.

This group appears to be in general alignment with the FAA and other governing officials. Its principles are:

1.   Safe and competent use of drones: Drones, like any tool such as a car or hammer, have some risks associated with their use. We seek to operate our equipment in a manner that does not threaten anyone's safety, person, or privacy. Educating our membership about safe and respectful practices is a core part of our mission.

2.   Legal use of drones: Although we may not agree with many of the current regulations, we also believe in following the law of the land.

3.   Humane use of drones: We like our flying robots to help people, not hurt them, and we are always seeking new ways to use our drones that will have a positive impact in our society (Charter of the United Nations-Preamble, 2014, para 6).

At the meeting, the investigator presented the tabletop briefing and discussed the research project to elicit feedback from this stakeholder group. The majority of the participants at this meeting were highly educated (bachelor's and master's degree holders) with many years of experience in the small drone marketplace. Many of the participants were actively seeking to operate commercial UAV businesses. They also made it clear to the investigator they did not specifically speak for the Drone Users Group Network. Many individuals within this stakeholder group (marketplace) are craving for self-leadership that will allow UAVs into the NAS. The group enthusiastically discussed and embraced the research project; they expressed great frustration with the long and difficult process to allow a UAV to fly in the NAS (Mumm, 2014).

The group discussed its many attempts to work within the legal framework of the FAA regulations; however, after more than fifteen years of waiting, they have witnessed little progress toward commercial integration. The organizational and leadership aspects that group members discussed appeared to indicate that the group feels that they have little or no say in the process. Also, the process is impeding their ability to own and operate successful UAV production or services business. The Drone User Group Network promotes using drones for the good of all. They currently offer:

"A $10,000 prize for the most socially beneficial, documented use of a drone platform costing less than $3,000. Through this prize, we hope to spur innovation, investment and attention to the positive role that civilian drone technology can play in our society. We believe that flying robots are a technology with tremendous potential to make our world a better place, and we are excited that they are cheap and accessible enough that regular people and community groups can have their own," (Charter of the United Nations-Preamble, 2014).

Another participant invited the investigator to the UAS Test Site Luncheon. By attending this event, the investigator gained a perspective into the UAS test sites and activities. Although the FAA awards and endorses the UAS test sites, they are not necessarily funding these sites or activities. This luncheon featured the directors of the UAS test sites from Fairbanks University in Fairbanks, Alaska and Virginia Tech in Blacksburg, Virginia.

At this luncheon, Craig Woolsey, the Director for the Virginia Center for Autonomous Systems at Virginia Tech (VT) discussed the Mid-Atlantic Aviation Partnership (MAAP) between the Commonwealth of Virginia and the State of New Jersey. The MAAP also cooperates with the University of Maryland as the partnership seeks to apply ongoing research to known data points to assist the FAA in the safe integration of UAVs into the NAS.

During this discussion, Woolsey outlined how VT operates its test center. This includes the boundaries within which the UAVs fly at the test center. In addition, Woolsey stated that VT flies UAVs in the NAS in order to gather data necessary to help regulatory bodies make decisions on the use of UAVs in the NAS (Mumm, 2014). The investigator has studied research that discusses initially operating UAVs in Class E and Class G open airspace extensively. The VT test center appears to be taking the opposite approach; it has waivers that exempt its activities from Virginian legislation as well as the current FAA decisions. The legislation issue is briefly touched on in a publication that states,

"In response to a perceived policy vacuum concerning the use of UAS, Virginia became the first state in the nation to codify UAV legislation with a two-year moratorium limiting UAS access to the national airspace...As the policy environment surrounding UAS matures, the Virginian General Assembly is tasked with balancing privacy, safety and a considerable economic stake in this emerging industry," (*The Future of Unmanned Vehicle Systems in Virginia*, 2014, p. 2).

The Commonwealth of Virginia offers that by creating a restrictive environment for emerging technologies, they are providing leadership in the emerging technology field of UAS. This idea may not support their cause, as a permissive environment tempered by logical restriction would allow leadership to assist the self-organizing entities in this field fly safely and collect the necessary data faster and more economical. This creates an inclusionary environment, as illustrated in the press on a daily basis; the time has long since passed that the FAA or Virginia legislators can stop the forward momentum of the industry. Attending drone user groups and other open-forum meetings, or "fly ins," makes this fact clear to the investigator. The adaptation of the complexity theory in this case would allow the self-organizing entities, such as the drone user groups, the autonomy tempered with guidance from the FAA to assist in creating a solution to the current issues of allowing UAVs into the NAS.

Across the country, one can find this level of industry and state governance momentum. "In 2013, forty-three states introduced 130 bills and resolutions addressing UAS issues. At the end of the year, thirteen states had enacted sixteen new laws and eleven states had adopted sixteen resolutions" ("Unmanned Aircraft Systems (UAS) Legislation-2013," 2014, para 1). As shown in Figure 18, eight states have not yet introduced any UAS legislation, further exacerbating the nation's struggle. Time is not on the side of the legislators—many individuals and companies already own and fly drones. It may be too late to show leadership on this issue. The best that the legislators can hope for is a balance between the promise of future laws and the showdowns that are occurring almost every day. After years of waiting, UAV operators are openly flying in the NAS without the blessing from the FAA or their state legislature.

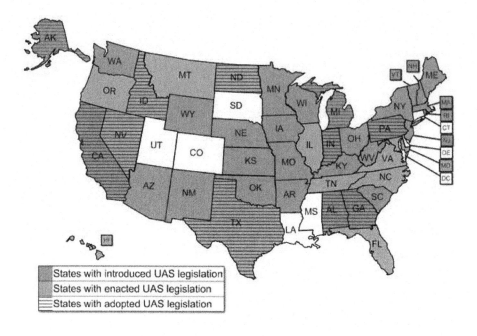

Figure 18 - Comparison of State UAS Legislations Activities

Recently, Jim Williams, the head of the FAA Unmanned Aircraft Systems Office, spoke at the semi-annual AUVSI organization meeting concerning the path forward for some UAV specific missions. Williams stated:

"Some of the commercial applications the FAA is expected to allow prior to finalizing the rules include UAS power line inspections and filmmaking. AUVSI and other groups, along with UAS manufacturers such as Yamaha, have been critical of the agency's slow progress with integrating unmanned aircraft into the National Airspace System... Companies from four industries have approached the FAA and are considering filing exemption requests, which would begin the process... The work using Section 333 to authorize some UAS operations, is just beginning. I want to be sure that it is clear that the operations we are talking about are specific, limited, and low-risk to people and property on the ground," (Bellamy, 2014,para 3-6)have been critical of the agency's slow progress with integrating unmanned aircraft into the National Airspace System (NAS.

Williams' statement refers to Section 333 of the *FAA Modernization and Reform Act of 2012*. This act contradicts other laws regarding U.S. citizens' property rights. According to property laws cited here, the property owners in the United States own the "non- navigable" airspace above their land.

"The United States Congress and the courts clarified the scope of landowners' airspace rights in the early twentieth century when airplanes began taking to the skies. Federal legislation enacted during that period carefully defined 'navigable airspace,' which generally encompasses all space situated more than 500 feet above the ground, and designated that space as a nationally-shared common area for modern flight," (Rule, 2012, pp. 427-428).

The actual limitation is the "minimum safe altitude" as defined by the FAA. In some cases, the minimum safe altitude can extend up to 1,000 feet above the highest obstacle and within 2,000 feet of the aircraft over congested areas.

PRESENTATION AND DISCUSSION OF FINDINGS

The goal for the interview sample was 20 SMEs. Although this may appear to be a low sample size, this is an emerging industry with many different components and issues. There are relatively few SMEs with a broad and deep understanding of the industry to create a representative sample. Almost all of the SMEs contacted for interviews were receptive; however, two of the SMEs who agreed to the interview were non-responsive to specific requests for in-person appointment times or over the phone interviews. These SMEs were replaced by other individuals from the same organizations with the same function. In-person interviews accounted for 80% (sixteen of the twenty) interviews. Four of the SMEs were geographically distant from the researcher. Since this was self-funded research effort, these four interviews took place via telephone.

The range of emotions exhibited by the participants during the in-person interviews surprised the investigator. At one end, participants displayed blood pressure-raising frustration when discussing the current situation in the UAV industry. At the other end, a participant despaired because a UAV company in which he invested 15 years ago soon will declare bankruptcy. Both spectrums displayed responding to the lack of rules and regulations allowing UAVs to fly in the NAS. Participants also showed excitement akin to opening up presents on Christmas morning when discussing the promise of the UAV industry with its potential for positive influence on all human kind. New adventures wait with every new UAV opportunity. The interviews offered the human side to the issues discussed. Several participants expressed a need for leadership and a desire for an industry to lead into the future. Near-violent reactions occurred when discussing bureaucratic hurdles. Many showed utter disappointment regarding investments in an industry with so much promise, yet so much chaos. Several participants had served in the U.S. military and demonstrated a "patriotic" emotionalism. Participants suggested that the U.S. government actively permits competitive countries and enemies of the U.S. to outpace the U.S. in the UAV industry. They suggested the bureaucratic notion of the past supports their argument in allowing the U.S. to fall behind in the UAV industry. Trust is a key component of leadership and many participants do not trust what is occurring; they do not trust that the leadership is truly making decisions in the best interest of all involved.

Voice inflections from the phone interview participants mirrored the wide range of emotions demonstrated in person. The one-on-one interviews took place in offices and restaurants that provided a personal, non-threatening atmosphere. To build rapport, the investigator and participants discussed participants' experiences, hobbies, education, business and employment interests. The investigator also explained the CTU degree program. The participants were relaxed and the atmosphere was light, yet professional.

The interviews continued with the tabletop briefing. The participants appeared receptive, and even hopeful, as the investigator explained the purpose and scope of the research. A noticeable shift in body language, emotions and facial expressions occurred as the investigator presented the tabletop briefing (Appendix B) that outlined the current situation. Participants showed clear frustration, and sometimes hopelessness, when discussing the current leadership and organizational issues surrounding the integration of UAVs into the NAS. One participant showed his frustration stating that because of the leadership and organizational challenges that have plagued the FAA and the federal government, he will take his UAV business offshore. He said that he has waited for close to fifteen years for the FAA "to get its act together" and they have failed repeatedly. The terms frustrated, angry, disappointed, fed up, clueless, bureaucratic nonsense, out of control organization, and an organization void of leadership and direction illustrated the emotions of this participant. Other participants were neutral during this stage of the tabletop briefing offering encouragement, ideas, and additional resources to the investigator to enhance the research and ensure research accuracy. Other participants did not appear to have personal finances at stake; they had their reputations at stake and they all felt they should consider the safety of the public.

Discussing complexity theory and its role in the research kept all participants actively engaged. The participants generally understood complexity theory and had some knowledge of chaos theory. This helped frame the research and heightened the participants' curiosity on how these theories and ideas could be adapted to leadership and organizational change models. The participants discussed several traits of a successful leader such as integrity, shared vision and action, caring, engaging, communication, collaboration, transition and empowerment. The need for organizational change was a deep-seated frustration.

Some of the SMEs discussed the history of flight and the FAA. Not all of the participants agreed that experimentation was the only path to growth. A few participants believed that the current process, however long and arduous, serves a purpose, however, most participants did not agree with this assessment. One participant looked back in history and commented that if the Wright brothers, or any other early adopter of aviation technology, had to deal with the FAA and the U.S. government's bureaucracy, we would all still be riding horses.

Recap of Data Analysis

The data collection for this study came from twenty SMEs that included the FAA and the UAV community. Participants' statements, recommendations, suggestions, and documents provided after the interviews provided additional data. There was a strong positive response to using the complexity leadership model to provide tangible momentum to the UAV integration into the NAS process. The primary caveat was the likelihood of the FAA would not be able to execute the process with their current structure. The FAA was significantly more optimistic that they could adapt their processes and resources to this methodology.

In order to adapt the complexity model into a leadership and organizational change model, training must occur. The concept can be difficult for people to understand and implement in real world situations. For most participants, implementing the complexity leadership model presented the most difficulty. Only answering the outside organization execution model question provided the participants confidence in the ability to execute this complexity model. Responding to the interviewees' suggestions for additional data gathering, the investigator ascertained that the FAA is already pushing a significant portion of the responsibility for the integration process off to the newly chosen UAS test sites. The FAA has given UAS test sites COA authority and airworthiness approval for UAV operators and manufacturers that come to them with their aircraft and the requisite fee.

Critical leadership issues went well beyond the FAA to (a) Congress, (b) the federal bureaucratic rulemaking process, (c) the powerful stakeholders, and (d) the lack of representation from the small user community and manufacturers. Participants also expressed that several key stakeholders felt shut out being offered no role in the process. Participants did not give consideration to small businesses, UAV operators, private organizations that fly UAVs for the public good (akin to the Civil Air Patrol) and smaller stakeholders. Public stakeholders only received consideration in the rulemaking process during the comment phase, which comes toward the process' end. Almost all participants acknowledged that the public was already operating at a constituent force forcing function at the state level for UAV laws.

Several unexpected findings arose during the interview process. For example, the timeline for the federal rulemaking process could prove to be the downfall of the entire process. The democratic process as a whole is slow and purpose driven; it is deliberate and deliberately slow. This idea works well when considering a Constitutional Amendment, however, not in the technology world. In the days when committees could only meet once every six months due to travel restrictions, or it took two weeks to mail documents to the committee members, the current rulemaking process might have worked well. Figure 19 provides a flow chart depicting the beginning of the rulemaking process. This flow chart shows the steps that are required for the FAA ARC to come up with a recommendation. If approved, the recommendation moves forward into the five-year rulemaking processes. If rejected, the process starts over.

This first process is an onerous process; however, it pales in comparison to the full rulemaking process that takes over when the first process ends. Appendix E provides a depiction of the steps that the FAA must execute to reach the final rule or regulation. This process' timeliness has received careful study. A simple rule, with little or no contention, takes five years to complete the process. This does not include the time it takes the FAA to create its recommendations for said rule. The rulemaking process for UAVs is not likely to be simple or without contention. Because UAV rules will have an economic impact of more than $100 million, the rules may be subject to economic impact and environmental impact studies that increase the time in making a final decision. The FAA is running out of time regarding the UAV community.

COMMITTEE FLOWCHART

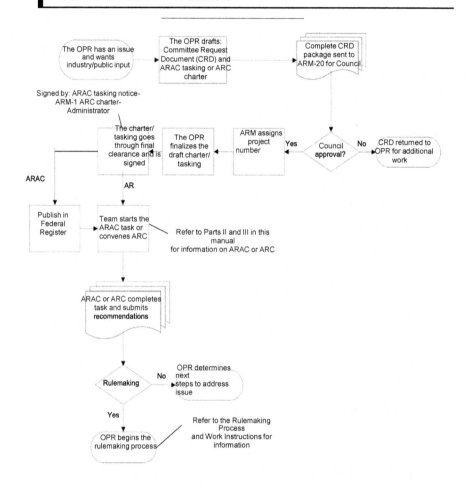

Figure 19 - Rulemaking Process (Humphries, 2013)

The rulemaking process is a systemic problem throughout the government. The process, designed to be slow, allows for more inclusion into the final product while addressing all of the Congressional requirements. The process can reduce the goal of inclusion until near the end of the process. If there are problems discovered at this point, the process has to go back three steps and begin preparation of the revised rule. As contentious as the UAVs rules might be, following this method could put the FAA in a rulemaking loop. In an industry moving in microseconds, a five-year process could hinder the United States' ability to compete.

The FAA's ultralight aircraft and radio-controlled aircraft management represents a possible game-changing opportunity to handling the UAV integration process. Incorporating the complexity leadership model into a similar process would create an easier, and faster, path forward. The Pirker court decision (Levin, 2014) is just starting to ripple through the UAV community. Some are taking advantage of it, but most are waiting to see the outcome of the appeal. If the appeal upholds the ruling, all eyes will shift to Congress to see if they pass a law to allow the FAA to regulate UAVs. Perhaps they will allow the community and the FAA to work out the solution free of the federal rulemaking process.

CHAPTER SUMMARY

The data collected indicates strong support for applying complexity theory to a leadership and change management model. Most participants believe that it could assist the integration of UAVs into the NAS. There was no consensus on specifically applying the complexity theory to the problem, but there was strong support for outsourcing the solution to an organization, or multiple organizations, outside the FAA. This research sought to expand theories and to offer new ways of examining the problem set, not specific solutions to all of the issues concerning the integration and harmonization of UAVs in the NAS. Significant disagreement regarding how to integrate UAVs into the NAS exists; however, all parties agree that safe UAV flight, with the accessibility to the NAS for the success of all involved is the goal. Additional analysis involving how the demographic of the participants may have affected the views of the participants is beyond the scope of the findings presented here. This line of inquiry is available, however, to dig deeper into the subject of human behavior and the correlation or lack of correlation with the collected demographical data.

Two underlying questions that go to the heart of the problem emerged. How safe is safe enough? How much data do you need to make the individual recommendations to allow UAVs into the NAS? FAA manned aircraft safety requirements rules measure fatal accidents: 100,000 departures or accidents per 1,000,000 passenger miles (National Policy-Flight Standards Service Oversight-order 800.368A, 2012). UAV research does not provide this type of data readily. Gathering this style of data would require extensive time. The UAV community suggests that a few simple rules, such as avoiding airports and major population centers, presents acceptable risk, requires little data collection to initiate operations, and provides for the small UAVs (Mumm, 2014).

The schism outlined here has set the stage for a significant amount of conflict between the FAA and the UAV community. A significant portion of the UAV community states that their voice is not part of the process. Also, the fact that the process has taken so long with no a target date in sight creates frustration (Mumm, 2014). The information collected in this study illustrates the frustration of all involved in this emerging industry. Not all parties are moving in the same direction and many parties to this industry feel that they have no ability to influence the process or outcome.

The research uncovered a significant impediment to the implementation of a complexity-style leadership model. The linear, authoritarian, onerous rulemaking process threatens to prevent any timely solution rule set from coming out of the FAA, no matter how dedicated the personnel. Given the responses working within the current process, the complexity model could increase the participation of the stakeholders, reduce conflict, and arrive at a good proposed rule set significantly sooner than the current timeline; however, the basic, overall timeframe would still be governed by the rulemaking process.

As innovators in this emerging industry, leaders must learn that the creativity to overcome obstacles rises up out of adversity and frustration.

There will be setbacks, but setbacks are an inevitable part of innovation and adaptation. Leaders must show the courage of their convictions and be steady in the darkest hours. As innovators, leaders must strive to find the methods that will launch the dreams and success of an industry, a company, or an individual person. Moving from linear thought processes to complexity theory processes presents challenges. It also creates processes that launch dreams of a company, a country or an individual. It allows leaders to guide from a distance with emerging behaviors that move toward the goals from dreams to reality.

Attitude reflects leadership. Study participants demonstrated an attitude of resigned defeat with no regard to loss of confidence in the process, economic loss, opportunity loss or the possibility of loss of life due to inaction. Loss of life is becoming a reality. One example occurred March 6, 2013 as a "passenger aircraft has near miss with drone above New York," (Humphries, 2013, para).

Leaders take risks. Leaders must be creative based upon either their experience or their lack of understanding of situations. Sometimes innovation is stifled because of bureaucracy. The research results illustrate that it may be possible to use the complexity theory as a new leadership and change management tool to manage the integration and harmonization of UAVs into the NAS.

CHAPTER EIGHT

"Abandon the urge to simplify everything, to look for formulas and easy answers, and to begin to think multidimensionally, to glory in the mystery and paradoxes of life, not to be dismayed by the multitude of causes and consequences that are inherent in each experience – to appreciate the fact that life is complex."

– M. Scott Peck (M. S. Peck, 1998, p. 14)

CONCLUSIONS

The key to original research is if the research added to the book of knowledge for humanity. This book and the research study reported in it adds to the book of knowledge as it creates a leadership framework by using an expansion of complexity theory that generates an innovative approach to a leadership and management structure. Using this structure will expeditiously integrate UAVs into the NAS to perform a multitude of missions, including commercial, homeland security and humanitarian activities. This management structure appears to succeed because the leadership framework that embraces a non-linear design encourages the disparate organizations to come together in a cooperative fashion and solve intersecting issues for the benefit of all stakeholders.

The research and findings presented in this book provide evidence that using an adaptation of the complexity theory coupled with leadership and organizational change models offer a potential way to move away from the slow, linear and authoritarian framework to a more rapid, inclusive and collaborative environment. A discussion and review of the research findings, the implications of the research, the research limitations and the conclusions offer final insights on leadership, organizational change, and how to leverage the complexity theory in future models and frameworks. All stakeholders generally desire the same outcome, even though each stakeholder is looking at the issues through a different lens and the stakeholders have differing individual goals.

This chapter presents the (a) findings, (b) limitations of the study, (c) implications of research, (d) implications of study, (e) recommendations for future research, and (f) researcher reflections and conclusions. This chapter describes the study's implications regarding a potential change in the fields of leadership and organizational change management execution based on the use of complexity theory as an adaptive approach focused on the need to lead people through a highly complex problem solving process. Human behavior models, organizational change and organizational group dynamics, coupled with changing leadership roles and the theory of self-organizing entities and boundary controls, are discussed in the context of the research questions and the associated findings. Inclusion, cooperation, and coordination within an active social system will be required to create positive long-term change to integrate and harmonize UAVs into the NAS. The literature review, the research findings, and the frustration level of most stakeholders paint a consistent picture. The vast majority of the research appears to illustrate that the current linear, authoritarian leadership and organizational processes do not work well when it comes to the integration and harmonization of unmanned and manned systems within the national airspace. Resisting change is not a new phenomenon. In this case, the investigator noted that the resistance does not result from a single action from the FAA employees, the contractors, the aviation industry, or the research and development community. The resistance to organizational and performance-based change arises from the leadership process within the government structure. Successful leadership behavior is often a calculated risk integrated with intellect and a break from the past without discounting the lessons of the past.

RESEARCH RESULTS

Complexity style change management matches the problem of integrating UAVs into the NAS. Its potential use received strong support across the spectrum of SMEs involved in the study. Although UAVs are seemingly just a new type of aircraft that need to be blended in with existing manned aircraft, the multitude of issues and stakeholders have shown the current linear, authoritarian leadership process to be inadequate and ill-matched to the pace of change that the majority of stakeholders demand.

The study's three research questions provided the research impetus. The first research question, how might the FAA employ a complexity style of change management to integrate UAVs into the NAS, proved to be the most difficult question for both the SME interviewees and the investigator. The FAA is exercising significant creativity through their UAS test site program and UAS centers of excellence. The fact that the federal government rulemaking process drives the FAA's leadership method creates the challenge. This process is rigid, linear, authoritarian, time-consuming and prone to a recursive-loop where the solution never emerges. The FAA team responsible for the integration of UAVs into the NAS is surprisingly small compared to the task. The FAA team has wisely outsourced portions of the problem; however, the groups involved in the outsourcing are following the rulemaking template for sophisticated manned commercial aircraft. The result has been a clear mismatch with the UAV paradigm. It became apparent during the interview process that the FAA would have to take the outsourcing effort to a new level—a level that would operate outside of the federal government rulemaking process.

There is precedence for operating outside the rulemaking process in three different ways. The first way is for Congress to grant the FAA with a waiver so they do not have to comply with some or all of the federal rulemaking laws. The second approach is for the FAA, with either internal or with external assistance, to create a voluntary rule set similar to those governing the RC model aircraft community. This approach provides the FAA with the flexibility to create piecemeal rules that can apply to different UAV capability levels and that can evolve relatively quickly over time. The third way is for the FAA to allow the UAV community to self-regulate, as the FAA does with the ultra-light aircraft community. All three of these methods would enable the FAA to operate outside of the federal government rulemaking process and could facilitate the use of a complexity style of change management.

The second question: Could the employment of a complexity style of change management expedite the integration of UAVs into the NAS? This question generally received an affirmative response. It was broadly felt that the use of a complexity style of change management, if executed properly, could arrive at a solution for UAV integration, which would be acceptable to all or nearly all of the stakeholders, allowing rapid integration of this solution for the success of all involved. The interviewed SMEs all supported the appropriate inclusiveness of the different stakeholders when addressing the different integration issues. The current process addresses only a couple of issues at a time using the linear style of solving one problem to help address the next problem. The federal rulemaking process further exacerbates this time-consuming approach. Both the participants and the investigator noticed that many interdependent issues exist; the most expeditious path would address all of the issues in parallel using a complexity model. The logistics associated with executing the complexity model process though group meetings concerned the participants. The region around the nation's capital has access to SMEs and representatives in all of the stakeholder categories. Additionally, the UAV community meets twice a year at AUVSI events for the better part of a week. A few of the stakeholders would require special invitations since they do not typically attend these events.

The FAA could use the answers that emerge from the capacity and the complexity tool to expedite the overall process. If the FAA chooses to use the emergent answers to feed the normal federal rulemaking process, then modest efficiency gains are possible. Significant acceleration in the process could occur if the FAA chooses to use the emergent answers to create a voluntary rule set. It is likely that the emergent answers will contain one or more logistical requirements, such as registration, course completions, and flight plan filing. How the FAA chooses to address that additional workload will also influence the pace of integration of UAVs into the NAS. The FAA's limited staff could create a bottleneck when trying to execute these logistical requirements. The FAA could choose to outsource the logistical requirements to expedite the process further. The bottom line for this research question is that use of the complexity style of change management is essential to expedite the integration process. The potential benefits are difficult to calculate because it is not clear how the FAA will use the emergent answers from the process and how they execute any logistical requirements.

The third research question: What are the critical leadership issues impeding the movement of UAVs into the NAS? This question elicited both systemic and altruistic-based responses. The first systemic issue is the impact of the federal rulemaking process on the FAA leadership decisions. This process is linear, constrictive, inflexible, and authoritarian in nature. As such, it restricts the potential for FAA's leadership to solve the UAV integration challenge. The FAA has found creative ways to advance their mission despite the federal rulemaking process limitations of the speed of change—even though the FAA tends to use the process to make changes in the operations that they govern. Historically, the federal rulemaking process has served the FAA well because the vast majority of their current stakeholders are change adverse. When the FAA makes safety or capacity-related changes, it often creates a financial burden for the current set of stakeholders or at least increases the level of inconvenience to the current stakeholders.

The second systemic problem revolves around seats at the rulemaking table. The number of seats is limited, limiting the true range of stakeholders that are able to participate, and overloading the table with government and government-contractor power-players. This arrangement pushes the commercial operators and the small manufacturing companies to the sidelines despite the fact that they are the primary groups impacted by any new set of FAA rules. The participants in the study repeatedly raised this issue. The third systemic problem is the missing stakeholders. These absent stakeholders include (a) the Federal Communications Commission (FCC), (b) data link companies, (c) insurance companies, (d) the purchasers of UAV services community, (e) the local law enforcement community, (f) the first responders community, (g) the non-military/NASA government user community, (h) the legal torte community, (i) toy companies, (j) the RC aircraft community, and (k) the public.

The majority of the altruistic issues were anti-altruistic. The first of these issues is that every stakeholder group has an agenda and not all of these agenda are pro-UAV. The airline operator/pilot community, the general aviation pilot community, and the fourth amendment public community are less than enthusiastic about UAV proliferation into the NAS. The political community tends to focus on jobs, votes, and fundraising. With UAVs, these activities can conflict. UAV enthusiasts want to fly their UAVs and the public is concerned with privacy rights. These issues do not always align with jobs, votes, or fundraising. A vocal portion of the public stakeholder group expresses concern about fourth amendment privacy rights. Existing laws, such as "Peeping Tom" laws, would cover UAVs; however, challenges arise in associating a person to a UAV intrusion. This issue becomes more complicated as toys and UAVs begin to overlap. While UAV operators likely will act in a professional manner, toy users may not. Government and law enforcement also present another major fourth amendment concern. Laws and procedures exist that frame this privacy use issue; the concern lies when wondering whether law enforcement and the government will honor them. Law enforcement and the government have legal waivers and other means to work around existing laws. The use of UAVs could proliferate due to their lower cost compared to federally acquired helicopters and fixed wing aircraft; the government could cross their ethically acceptable boundaries. Moving in the opposite direction and acting on fear, however, has caused several state and local government to work toward creating anti-UAV laws.

Several leadership issues remain relating to how the FAA handles risk. Even when establishing and executing proper risk mitigation strategies, leadership must accept some residual risk. For the last several decades, the FAA's primary focus has been on the process to wring out as much risk as possible from the aviation community and especially the airline transport operations. They have succeeded. "Last year, an MIT statistics professor determined that ⊠the death risk' for passengers of commercial airlines is one in 45 million flights" (Jacobs, 2013, para 3). Ironically, that success now impedes the FAA's desire to take on the potential additional risk that UAVs present to safe operations in the NAS. The next leadership issue for the FAA is reputation. The FAA's reputation is decades in the making; the hallmark of making very few mistakes although the mistakes that are made create lessons learned that allow the FAA to continue to strive toward "perfection." This level of quality control is difficult to maintain with the addition of large numbers of new UAV aviation assets. UAVs have a wide variety of designs and missions. Limited test data exists to support the stringent safety record the FAA requires. Compounding the issue further is hundreds, if not thousands, of products with a wide range of capabilities, sizes, and configurations beginning to enter the NAS over a short time. This concern often leads the leadership to stifle the integration process so much that it stagnates.

LIMITATIONS OF THE STUDY

The investigator encountered several limitations that do not appear to have affected the initial research. These limitations included funding, willing and available participants, technology, and the speed and volume of newly published, relevant data.

Funding was one of the more critical limitations of this research; the investigator self-funded this research. In order to continue this investigation, the investigator must invest a substantial amount of time and travel to increase the pool of research participants. The field of UAVs is still an emerging technology area with few SMEs on whom to lean for guidance. This limits the geographically available interview pool and has the possibility to skew data collection results slightly, as the industry continues to change, grow and adapt to changing circumstances.

Future collaboration with other academics in the field of leadership research and organizational change models will allow this research to work toward expanded theories of human behavior models and advanced organizational change models. The funding, time, and overall resource limitations placed on the investigator did not allow for extensive collaboration.

The investigator took actions to ensure that all of the interviews were identical, whether conducted by phone or in person. The investigator has experience in leading organizational change through leadership roles. During the interviews, the investigator felt the frustration and the hopelessness of many of the participants. Minimizing bias to such a level that it is not an influence in the research study causes challenges and limitations in all research. The investigator relied on his extensive experience with leadership models, human factors models and organizational change models to provide a baseline to the investigation.

Resolutions to the challenges posed by UAVs appear reachable by conventional leadership methods and technology until one discovers that the human behavior, not technology, is the issue. Much information exists on the field of leadership and organizational change. The volume of research on how to lead people and organizations when faced with disruptive technology, however, appears sparse. The apparent near-term need for this new type of leadership and organizational change research created a study limitation. It also provided increased validity to this study. Due to the timeliness of the problem set and the strong forces involved, the research had to remain on a tight schedule. This kept the study relevant and timely at this key juncture in the UAV integration effort. Leadership and change management models need to match the speed of industry. The investigator and all of the participants agreed that the days of rulemaking committees taking over five years to make a decision should end, however, there is no champion coming forward to lead the charge for change. Due to the large mismatch between the government and the stakeholders, the government purposely made the pace of the process slow, with time to consider all angles of issues and unintended consequences. At the time, this thought process was logical; however, the lawmakers did not consider either the innovative issues of future technology or the speed of technology innovation cycles. The process should evolve to consider how the world will look in a hundred years. This perspective will consider the increasing pace of technology. The government purposely making the pace of the process slow does not provide a long-term solution. The complexity model, properly implemented, can eliminate this mismatch and lead to an accelerated process that produces a more informed result.

The rapid pace of media reports, research reports, technological breakthroughs, and breaking news stories limited the ability of the researcher to illustrate a true picture in time. The investigator set an information cutoff date in the original proposal because of this ongoing stream of new reporting related to UAVs.

Using the tri-coding method mitigated bias. The limitations in conducting phone interviews, having multiple coders review the same source data for accuracy, establishing a media cutoff date and utilizing version controls kept the data secure and in order and available for use in multiple locations.

IMPLICATIONS OF RESEARCH

This research applies directly to the study of leadership and organizational change. The conventional wisdom in these fields tends to default to linear and authoritarian approaches, including checklists. This provides control to the organizational structure, but it suppresses creativity and discourages the formation of self-organizing entities.

In a complexity-type system, each part of the system has part of the solution. All of the relevant stakeholders need to collaborate and coordinate on their part of the solution. Organizations tend to be chaotic, uncontrollable, and weak when responding to genuinely new situations; the FAA is no different. The complexity model of leadership offers learning, understanding, and positive results that do not appear achievable in the organization's current configuration. This would depart from the linear and authoritarian nature of the current leadership and organization of the FAA. Complexity theory leadership is both powerful and flexible.

Reacting to new situations takes time. Technological, business and societal changes are moving at a much faster pace than government legacy processes can manage. The current process has the leadership "hoping" that the organization will learn and create strategies to deal with the new conditions. This is a weakness of a linear authoritarian approach. Fear of authority, hoping for a positive outcome, and the sluggishness of required outcomes are all 180 degrees different in a complexity leadership model. Complexity leadership offers collaboration, inclusion and the ability to adjust speed to the situation and the recognition that not all issues are of the same importance to all stakeholders at the same frequency or depth in any given situation.

Although the FAA has employees and contractors across the United States, it does not appear that they are leveraging this network to reach out to the UAV community. Integrating and executing a complexity style of leadership may not be as difficult as it seems. The lack of UAV flight data is one of the key issues preventing the FAA from performing their normal safety analyses (Mumm, 2014). Interestingly, that the FAA could plug into the existing self-organized entities, such as the drone user groups, to get this information. They quickly could learn the emerging lessons and behaviors of the members by collecting data points from the

UAV flights occurring all over the United States. The FAA could then build a reporting framework, conduct data point collections, and suggest safety procedures and minimum pilot experience standards to guide the self-organizing entities without forcing a linear or authoritarian approach into the process.

Enrolling these self-organized entities would allow the FAA to control the data point collection through specific enrollment criteria and reporting schemas. This type of self- registration and self-reporting works well for the National Weather Service (NWS). Passionate citizens register with the NWS and agree to report weather data in a specific format using standardized reporting criteria and equipment. These self-organized weather reporters pay for their equipment, training and reporting method. This system provides the NWS, and other entities, with the ability to report weather-related information down to the zip code in any state in the United States. Guiding this volunteer data collection group is a simple set of rules, not by authoritarian overregulation, and is extremely successful (Mumm, 2014).

Collaboration and coordination of policies, laws and strategies is only a starting place in a world that is moving so quickly that it does not appear that the governing bodies can maintain their ability to govern. This inability to govern and lead will create long periods of massive instability with short periods of stability and peace. These short periods of stability will allow human kind to reset its ethics, core believes, economies, countries and the outlook for the next generation. When the world is faced with push button decisions at the speed of light as it continues to allow machines to do more and more critical thinking for human kind without the benefit of intellect or leadership, human kind has set itself up for failure as these actions will lead to only one logical outcome - revolution. Whether human kind chooses to accept the concept or not of sustainability does not singularly rest upon any leader's ability to forecast the future, make agile decisions and or be unafraid of change.

Guiding distributed human intelligence in a way that produces non-linear emergent behaviors (answers to problems) can create the evolutionary solutions to hard problems. This leads people, teams and entities in a logical, rapid fashion in a world that demands efficiency and effectiveness at levels not seen historically. The complexity theory offers power through its non-linear, accelerated evolution that matches the restless and perpetual change occurring in today's technological world. This restless and perpetual change demonstrates a world changing in such a way that it is not possible for the current linear, authoritarian leadership and organizational change models to match the pace of change. This mismatch reaches beyond the pace of technology to the pace of our human interaction with the technology and the way leaders can manage during this time of creative change.

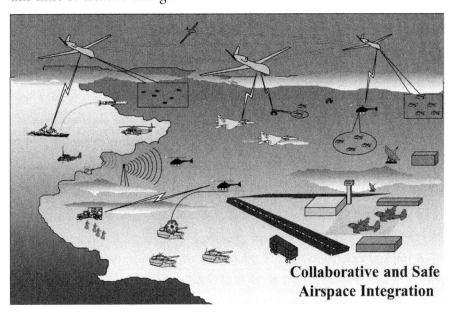

Figure 20 - Distributed Architecture

Adapting complexity theory to the fields of leadership and organizational change offers great promise including seeing the collaborative and safe airspace integration occur as depicted in figure 17. The world continues to move at an increasing pace. Information technology gives self-organizing entities the ability to emerge at will and bring solutions to issues at a speed never seen before. All human actions can have uncertain effects. Emerging solutions will occur as actions. The idea of creating technological and organizational change without risk is not leadership; it is also not logical. Leaders cannot know in advance the consequences of every decision. The leaders will not know how the environment around them will react to every decision. There is risk in all that humankind does; the real risk arises in continuing down a linear and authoritarian path of questionable means which will not lead to the future, but only hold onto the past.

Impact of Study on Leadership Models and Recommendations for Future Research

The current research expands existing theories and provides a foundation to create new theories in human behavior, leadership models and organizational change models. Future investigators may expand and continue research of several theories including (a) increasing complexity theory in a leadership and organizational change agent, (b) human behavior models, (c) organizational change and organizational group dynamics, (d) changing leadership roles and the theory of self-organizing entities and boundary controls.

A natural extension to this research is to superimpose the complexity theory leadership and change model onto the aviation rules and to the U.S. Government's rulemaking process (see Appendix E). This overlay offers the ability to use the power of the complexity theory, yet temper it with the general guidance of the rulemaking process. The self-organizing entities offer an outside-the-framework workspace, yet the general guidance offers the movement of all parties toward an end goal. Several organizational change theories, leadership theories, communication theories and authoritarian theories offer examination and thought into the research expansion.

The current problem set of the FAA may benefit from research using the action research methodology. Action research, as its name suggests, is action focused. Although thought provoking, the real value is in the action and feedback stages of this process. This type of research takes advantage of the cerebral employment of creating a hypothesis, researching to answer the hypothesis and then devising possible solutions. Action research then implements additional processes that allow the researcher to test the solutions in the real world. Once this step is completed, the researcher evaluates how well the hypothetical solution performed in the real world, then adjusts these solutions and the process starts over again.

This type of action injection and feedback mechanism may work well. The complexity theory adapted to the leadership and organizational change models requires a feedback loop that allows leaders and organizations the ability to be in a guiding role, not an authoritarian position. Stakeholder buy-in with a deeper comprehension of the issues likely will result. The complexity model takes advantage of the group as a whole for rules and organizational norms. Action research may allow the evolution of the complexity theory to adapt into the leadership role with the least amount of disruption as the change occurs. Several factors can offer challenges to this research. These factors include (a) outside pressures on leadership, (b) the ability of the organization to change in a logical, timely manner, (c) and the coordination and collaboration effort that intersecting agencies require.

A mixed-methods approach that combines qualitative and quantitative research would allow more angles of inquiry and may offer concrete ideas on conflict resolution, communication, human behavior modification, and complexity theory implementation. Different instruments allow for larger population pools. Quantitative results offer possible correlation points on the current leadership's effectiveness on issues such as the integration of UAVs into the NAS. This data could offer a correlation point as a before and after snapshot in time. If the FAA chooses to implement a complexity style of leadership, they could measure effectiveness and efficiencies in a variety of ways offering insight to the theory's ability to create positive change within an organization's leadership.

The concept of the FAA using a voluntary rule set modeled after how the FAA works with the radio controlled aircraft community or using an outside group to provide self-regulation of the UAV community as the FAA has done with the ultra-light aircraft community also warrants further study. Self-regulation does not mean zero-regulation; the UAV community would still need a rule set for guidance. The use of a complexity leadership model could be most effective and most expeditious in this rulemaking situation. The FAA stands as a key stakeholder in each of the issue groups instead of providing the tasking, approval and oversight authority. The FAA also would provide several roles in actual UAV flight operations and would provide feedback to the UAV community to provide better service both to UAVs and manned aircraft operating in the NAS.

CONCLUSION

The research has exposed the potential benefit of using the complexity style of leadership to accelerate the process of integrating UAVs into the NAS. The study also has brought out several key underlying issues that require innovative resolutions to create timely success for the FAA and the UAV community.

Complexity leadership theory recognizes there are not just two or three primary factors or stakeholders that need consideration in order to develop the "best" solution. There are many stakeholders and a myriad of key interactions that all need to meet a certain level of satisfaction. This makes it difficult for a single entity, such as the FAA, working with only a small subset of the stakeholders and issues, to achieve a solution in a timely fashion. Stakeholders and individuals need to work in a collaborative and structured environment in order to foster teamwork and achieve a unity of effort. This is not the standard consensus-building exercise that achieves the lowest common denominator. It presents a guided process that creates an emergent best, or near-best, solution that is, by its nature, inclusively achieved. Although several other leadership and management styles or systems are applicable to the UAV integration challenge, the research appears to support a complexity theory style of leadership and organizational change management as an excellent match for this situation.

Additional studies are justifiable in the use of complexity leadership theory for this challenge as well as other government, military and commercial challenges. Complex issues such as homeland security require timely solutions to protect American lives and freedom. Future research implementing the complexity leadership approach and innovative solutions to federal regulatory processes could offer leadership solutions that match the speed of human progress.

The evolving leadership and homeland security domain demands integrated social science approaches. They must contribute to the functional social developmental concepts of leadership and organizational change. They also must provide practical solutions to the challenging nature of human interaction. The integration of these research findings has direct relevance to the local, national and international development of leadership and organizational change management. Seen throughout history, human adaptation struggles as the pace of change quickens. This research offers yet another evolution into this adaptive nature. Applying decades of research in leadership, organizational change and human behavior sciences, the governance community can fill the knowledge gaps related to adaptive organizational and leadership challenges.

CHAPTER NINE

| Personal Reflections on Leadership

In analyzing the current situation, it does not appear that the leadership theories of the past will allow emerging industries to move intelligently into the future. The current leadership theories tend to answer questions in a linear fashion with questions of what do you have to do today to get where you want to go in the future. Although this is a good planning question, it tends to elicit simplistic answers. These answers do not fully account for today's complex world. Overlaying and integrating the complexity theory with different types of leadership and organizational change management theories may offer the ability to create the inclusive action necessary in this emerging industry.

In 51 BC, a great public speaker thought of himself as a leader. His name was Cicero. Cicero would give emotionally stirring speeches before large crowds. When he finished speaking, the crowds erupted in great cheers and applause (Lendering, 2013, para 9-16).

Another man lived at this time named Caesar. He also was a great public speaker and considered a leader in many people's eyes. Caesar would speak to the crowds after Cicero. Caesar spoke of greatness, of solutions to their ills, gave the people hope for a better tomorrow, and provided the leadership to make it so. When Caesar finished speaking, the crowds cheered with thunderous applause and then followed him. They marched with Caesar because they believed in his leadership and his direction (Lendering, 2013, para 9-24). The action that erupts when people believe in their leaders is unstoppable. The UAV community stakeholders are ready and willing to "march" to create dramatic changes; however, they need a Caesar to lead.

Another way of looking at this is, "The realization of your vision of career and life depends on the consequential actions you take or fail to take. A consequential action marks a point of no return," (Marichal, 2011, para 4). President Ronald Reagan said this slightly different as he said:

"The character that takes command in moments of crucial choices has already been determined by a thousand other choices made earlier in seemingly unimportant moments. It has been determined by all the 'little' choices of years past - by all those times when the voice of conscience was at war with the voice of temptation, [which was] whispering the lie that 'it really doesn't matter.' It has been determined by all the day-to-day decisions made when life seemed easy and crises seemed far away - the decision that, piece by piece, bit by bit, developed habits of discipline or of laziness; habits of self-sacrifice or self-indulgence; habits of duty and honor and integrity - or dishonor and shame," (Reagan, 1993).

As new leaders are trained to leave the old ways of authoritarian and linear thought processes behind, we must be cautious of sending these leaders back into organizations that are not ready for changes. Raelin says that, "You should never send a changed person back to an unchanged environment," (Raelin, 2004, p. 132).

Although the very concept of not sending a changed person back into an organization that needs to change seems illogical, some experts would argue for this course of action. The thought process behind sending people to an offsite meeting for leadership training is rooted in the issue that you do not want the person to be in familiar surroundings or always back at their desk not paying attention to the material. The gurus lean toward the idea that one person can make a difference, however, I think Raelin has it correct; unless the organization is ready (or forced by an outside influence or event) to change, one person will have little if any effect on the situation. Learning lists of attributes or activities that are supposed to create some super leader is just not realistic; leadership is not that easy. Now flying a plane, yes, pilots have checklists although in my twenty-three year of being a pilot I have found it is easier to fly a plane than to successfully lead people.

I also agree that depending on where in the organization a person is, affects their ability to create or implement change and this is the reason why it is critical to match the person to the appropriate level of leadership training. Sending a Private to the US Army War College will more than likely not create the desired results and the Private upon returning to his unit will not be an effective change agent.

Leadership training is essential for all levels; the key is to remember one of the leader's "critical roles is to find the right combination of inducements to get subordinates to do things. In fact, what makes a leadership presumably transformative is when this motivation is designed to get subordinates to do things altruistically on behalf of the wider organization," (Raelin, 2004, p. 132). I have found that one of the motivating factors for teams is training. The government typically talks about training as the most important item in a person's career, they will delay promotions if not all of the trainings have been completed, yet training is one of the first things that tends to get cut during a budget review.

As you read this book, I am hoping that you were thinking through how you could implement complexity leadership into your own life. As practitioners and leaders, we must study all sides of a given issue being mindful of our own bias on a given subject. Striving towards understanding and the greater good will work us in a direction of natural leadership and with luck, it will increase the probability that the future is better than present.

We also must collaborate and coordinate to consensus issues such as the integration of UAVs into the NAS. The world is moving so fast and what was important yesterday is not important today; this speed is driving change and we must guide this change with logic and understanding, not authoritarian and linear thought processes. This speed in gaining new experiences should help us make the world a better place as we strive not to repeat the mistakes of the past. This brings up one last issue. Are the mistakes of the past really mistakes? Can we not implement some of these so-called mistakes in the future with a successful outcome? Keeping in mind, almost every great invention or lead forward started with failure. Thomas Edison failed 1,000 times before he invented the light bulb. All research creates some amount of knowledge, through big data and other data mining techniques we can use information in new ways, so past failures can now lead us to future successes.

As leaders, we need work in think tanks, on boards and in the international arena to help senior officials understand the issues and make decisions. Congress has not kept up with technology or world events and thus they have not produced effective legislation and the legal frameworks for the future that could be applied to foreign soil or domestic spaces.

Congressional leaders must adapt a new mission and vision as well as react to world events and new technologies in a timely manner. They must integrate new technology faster and safer while being conscious of the legal, ethical, moral and constitutional aspects in securing the United States' innovation and thought leadership around the world.

When Congress and heads of states choose to not govern and control the important issues at hand and openly displays a lack of leadership and understanding of the world around us, the subordinates will define their own policies. If the leadership does not fully understand the issue, they become paralyzed in their decision-making capability. The internet and drones are two examples of Congress showing its ignorance. The first time lawmakers were interested in the internet was when they wanted to figure out a way to tax it. Congress failed to understand the entrepreneurial opportunities that would be created and thus Congress could not make decisions about the boundaries of the internet. BitCoin is only one example of what can happen when intellectual inspiration combines with unregulated freedoms. BitCoin is now running a billion dollar plus economy without the constraints or regulation of any government anywhere (Bitcoin is an innovative payment network and a new kind of money, 2015).

Congress understands that the drone policy issue both nationally and internationally illustrates the poor handling and understanding of new technology, as well as the implementation and integration into society. Our nation and our nation's enemies continuously modernize equipment and tactics used in wartime and peacetime to secure national interests. People, tanks, trucks, ships, missiles and planes have been the traditional tools of choice. The US has policies, doctrines, treaties, plans and procedures in place for dealing with the use and deployment of virtually all prior categories of war weapons, vehicles, and operators and their deployment in multiple scenarios.

The US needs to complete similar, sophisticated planning for unmanned vehicles and robotics. Yet, the US has neither prepared nor developed documentation or comprehensive plans to address the challenges presented by unmanned vehicles and robots on the modern battlefield or inside our borders. Throughout history, humans have accepted the inevitable loss of human life in war, in terrorist strikes, through political assassinations, in drug wars, as a result of crime, and natural disasters. Unmanned vehicles now are being developed to become remote killers of human beings. Given our advanced security, intelligence systems and weaponry; terrorist groups and other enemies will see the advantages of attacking the US using unmanned vehicles and robotics. This will make it far more difficult to identify the source of an attack. With very limited proliferation agreements, treaties and comprehensive technology tracking programs in place, responding effectively or planning preemptive action against these attacks will be difficult. The US and its allies will be threatened by terrorist groups, rogue nations and other non-state actors that have gained access to unmanned vehicles and robotic technologies that will be used against our national and international interests while the nation stands without a clear understanding of a necessary commitment and ability to strategically respond to such actions.

In examining the issues of complexity theory, we will need to step up and step out as leaders on the robotic technology forefront and provide a direction to governance and oversight communities who are not able to quickly adapt with the speed of change. The culture of linear and authoritarian leadership is not working and we must change this culture to one of inclusion, not exclusion. I agree with Starobin as he discusses the role of culture in leadership and societies. Starobin offers the idea that great civilizations rise and fall in a cyclical manner due to culture, not science, not the physics of gravitation or the size of an economy. Culture is the key (Starobin, 2009, pp. 75-77).

It is now our responsibility as academics, leaders and intellectuals to work towards a brighter future. The great thinkers of the past paved the way for us to get this far in history, it is now our responsibility to leave a better legacy for the next generation, implementing complexity leadership is an important step forward in this journey to enable a future that can respond to and adapt to a faster and more complex world.

APPENDIX A: REFERENCES

AATT National Airspace System Operational Concept Description-Volume I. (2003). National Air and Space Administration Retrieved from http://www.uavm.com/images/NASA_National_Airspace_Concept_Document_RTOFinal72_NASOCDV1. pdf#page=8&zoom=auto,0,455.

AATT National Airspace System Operational Concept Description (Volume I). (2003). National Air and Space Administration Retrieved from http://www.uavm.com/images/NASA_National_Airspace_Concept_Document_RTOFinal72_NASOCDV1. pdf#page=8&zoom=auto,0,455.

Acosta, J., & Diamond, J. (2015). U.S. intel worker blamed for White House drone crash. Retrieved March 5, 2015, from http://www. cnn.com/2015/01/26/politics/white-house-device-secret-service/

Basu, K., & Palazzo, G. (2008). Corporate Social Responsibility: A Process Model of Sensemaking. *Academy of Management Review, 33*(1), 122-136. doi: 10.5465/amr.2008.27745504

Bellamy, W. (2014, May 16, 2014). UAS Going Commercial in US? FAA Considers. *Avionics Today.* Retrieved May 18, 2014, from http://military.einnews.com/article/205125616/E7ooxkcJC-v0D5wH1?n=1&code=VB_zmrJfcKA9ITZJ

Bernstein, P. L. (1996). *Against the gods: The remarkable story of risk*: Wiley New York.

Bezuidenhout, C. N. (2012). Network-analysis approaches to deal with causal complexity in a supply network. *50*, 1840-1849. doi: 10.1080/00207543.2011.575088

Bitcoin is an innovative payment network and a new kind of money. (2015). Retrieved January 30, 2015, from https://bitcoin.org/en/

Bryman, A., & Bell, E. (2011). *Business Research Methods* (3rd ed.). Oxford, UK: Oxford University Press.

Burke, W. W. (1994). *Organization Development: A Process of Learning and Changing* (Second Edition ed.). Reading, Massachusetts: Addison-Wesley Publishing Company.

Caldwell, R. (2003). Models of Change Agency: a Fourfold Classification. *British Journal of Management, 14*(2), 131-142. doi: 10.1111/1467-8551.00270

Charter of the United Nations-Preamble. (2014). Retrieved May 11, 2014, from http://www.un.org/en/documents/charter/preamble.shtml

Cialdini, R. B. (2003). Crafting normative messages to protect the environment. *Current directions in psychological science, 12*(4), 105-109.

Congress. (2012). *PUBLIC LAW 112–95—FEB. 14, 2012.*

Connolly, B. (2014). When social media strategies go wrong. Retrieved May 20, 2014, from http://www.cio.com.au/article/545561/when_social_media_strategies_go_wrong/

Cooke-Davies, T., Cicmil, S., Crawford, L., & Richardson, K. (2007). We're Not in Kansas Anymore, Toto: Mapping The Strange Landscape of Complexity Theory, and Its Relationship to Project Managment. *Project Management Journal, 38*(2), 50-61.

Cornwell, L. (2013). Domestic Drones. Retrieved October 3, 2013, from http://www.kxan.com/news/states-consider-regulation-of-drones-in-us-skies_63252616

Creswell, J. W. (2009). *Research Design: Qualitative, Quantitative, and Mixed Methods Approaches.* Thousand Oaks, CA: Sage Publications.

Crichton, M. (2014). Michael Crichton Quotes. Retrieved May 8, 2014, from https://www.goodreads.com/author/quotes/5194.Michael_Crichton

Crossan, F. (2003). Research philosophy: towards an understanding. *Nurse Research, 11*(1), 46-55.

Cummings, T., & Worley, C. (2009). *Organization Development and Change* (M. Acuna Ed. Nineth Edition ed.). Mason, Ohio: South-Western Cengage Learning.

Dalamagkidis, K., Valavanis, K., & Piegl, L. (2008). On unmanned aircraft systems issues, challenges and operational restrictions preventing integration into the National Airspace System. *Progress in Aerospace Sciences, 44*(7), 503-519.

Daszko, M., & Sheinberg, S. (2005). Survival is optional: Only leaders with new knowledge can lead the transformation. *Transformation, 408*, 247-7757.

The Declaration of Independence. (2014). Retrieved March 8, 2015, from http://www.ushistory.org/declaration/document/index.htm

Dillow, C. (2013). Flying Solo. *Project Management Institute, 27*(7), 9-10.

DOT and FAA Propose New Rules for Small Unmanned Aircraft Systems. (2015). *Regulations will facilitate integration of small UAS into U.S. aviation system.* Retrieved March 5, 2015, from http://www.faa.gov/news/press_releases/news_story.cfm?newsId=18295

Egan, T. M. (2002). Grounded Theory Research and Theory Building. *Advances in developing human resources, 4*(3), 277-295.

Einstein, A. (2005). Albert Einstein Quotes. *Available at thinkexist.com.*

En Route Automation Modernization. (2013). Retrieved 10/11/2013, 2013, from http://www.faa.gov/air_traffic/technology/eram/

Expanding Use of Small Unmanned Aircraft Systems in the Arctic

Implementation Plan FAA Modernization and Reform Act of 2012. (2012). Washingon DC: Federal Aviation Adminstration Retrieved from http://www.faa.gov/about/initiatives/uas/media/suas_arctic_plan.pdf.

FAA. (2013). A Brief History of the FAA.

FAA Flight Plan-2009-2013. (2008). Washington, DC: Retrieved from http://www.faa.gov/about/plans_reports/media/flight_plan_2009-2013.pdf.

FAA Forms ARC to Reorganize Part 23. (2011, 8/25/2011). Retrieved 10/14/2013, 2013, from http://www.eaa.org/news/2011/2011-08-25_arc.asp

FAA Q&A Unmanned Aircraft (UAS). (2013). Retrieved 10/13/2013, 2013, from http://www.faa.gov/about/initiatives/uas/uas_faq/

FAA selects ITT for satellite-based ATC system. (2007). *Interavia Business & Technology*(689), 22-22.

The First Atomic Bomb Blast, 1945. (2003). Retrieved July 11, 2013, from http://www.eyewitnesstohistory.com/atomictest.htm

The Future of Unmanned Vehicle Systems in Virginia. (2014). Blacksburg, VA: Virginia Tech Office of Economic Development.

Gardberg, N. A. (2006). Reputatie, Reputation, Réputation, Reputazione, Ruf: A cross-cultural Qualitative Analysis of Construct and Instrument Equivalence. *Corporate Reputation Review, 9*(1), 39-61. doi: 10.1057/palgrave.crr.1550009

Germain, M.-L., Herzog, M. J. R., & Hamilton, P. R. (2012). Women employed in male-dominated industries: lessons learned from female aircraft pilots, pilots-in-training and mixed-gender flight instructors. *Human Resource Development International, 15*(4), 435-453. doi: 10.1080/13678868.2012.707528

Global Space Programs. (2012). Retrieved July 14, 2013, from http://www.spacefoundation.org/programs/public-policy-and-government-affairs/introduction-space/global-space-programs

Goppert, J., Liu, W., Shull, A., Sciandra, V., Hwang, I., & Aldridge, H. (2012). Numerical Analysis of Cyberattacks on Unmanned Aerial Systems. *American Institute of Aeronautics and Astronautics stated.*

Groenland, E. A. G. (2002). Qualitative Research to Validate the RQ-Dimensions. *Corporate Reputation Review, 4*(4), 308.

Grover, V., Seung Ryul, J., Kettinger, W. J., & Teng, J. T. C. (1995). The Implementation of Business Process Reengineering. *Journal of Management Information Systems, 12*(1), 109-144.

H.R. 1848: Small Airplane Revitalization Act of 2013. (2013). Washington DC: Retrieved from http://www.govtrack.us/congress/bills/113/hr1848/text
http://www.govtrack.us/congress/bills/113/hr1848/text/eh.

Hattotuwa, S. (2015). Non-Lethal UAV & Drones. Retrieved March 14, 2015, from https://flipboard.com/@sanjanah/non-lethal-uavs-%26-drones-vdfqmqt1y

Henning, J. C. (2012, February 20, 2012). Embracing the Drone, *The New York Times.* Retrieved from http://www.nytimes.com/2012/02/21/opinion/embracing-the-drone.html?pagewanted=all&_r=0

Heyes, J. D. (2013). Armed drones soon to be operated by dozens of countries; will they decide to strike U.S. targets? Retrieved July 14, 2013, from http://www.naturalnews.com/040910_armed_drones_drone_attacks_surveillance.html

Homeland Security: Boom and Bust-A Troubled History. (2010). Retrieved April 12, 2013, from http://www.publicintegrity.org/national-security/homeland-security/homeland-security-boom-and-bust

How many chickens are there in the United States? How many eggs do they produce? (2013). *Poultry Fact.* Retrieved November 21, 2013, from http://www.ansc.purdue.edu/faen/poultry%20facts.html

Hughes, D. (2006). Dawn of ADS-B. *Aviation Week & Space Technol-*

ogy, 164(19), 37-37.

Humphries, M. (2013). Passenger Aircraft has Near Miss with Drone Above New York.   Retrieved May 30, 2014, from http://www.geek.com/news/passenger-aircraft-has-near-miss-with-drone-above-new-york-1541945/

Hunt, J. G. (1996). *Leadership: A new synthesis*. Newbury Park, California: Sage Publications, Inc.

Introduction of the Unmanned Aerial Vehicles (UAVs). (2013). Retrieved July 21, 2013, from http://www.defense.gov/specials/uav2002/

Jacobs, P. (2013). 12 Reasons Why Flying Is The Safest Way To Travel. *Business Insider*, Pg 1 para 3. Retrieved from Business Insider website: http://www.businessinsider.com/flying-is-still-the-safest-way-to-travel-2013-7?op=1

Johnson, H. H., & Fredian, A. J. (1986). Simple Rules for Complex Change. *Training & Development Journal, 40*(8), 47.

Kim, A., Wampler, B., Goppert, J., Hwang, I., & Aldridge, H. (2012). Cyber Attack Vulnerabilities Analysis for Unmanned Aerial Vehicles. *The American Institute of Aeronautics and Astronautics: Reston, VA, USA.*

Konig, A., Kammerlander, N., & Enders, A. (2013). The Family Innovator's Dilemma: How Family Influences Affects the Adoption of Discontinuous Technologies by Incumbent Firms. *Academy of Management Review, 38*(3), 418-441. doi: 10.5465/amr.2011.0162

Koppenjan, J., & Klijn, E.-H. (2004). *Managing uncertainties in networks: Public private controversies*: Routledge.

Lee, Y.-K., & Chang, C.-T. (2010). Framing public policy: The impacts of political sophistication and nature of public policy. *The Social Science Journal, 47*(1), 69-89.

Lendering, J. (2013). Gaius Julius Caesar.   Retrieved July 8, 2014, from http://www.livius.org/caa-can/caesar/caesar01.html

Levin, A. (2014). Commercial Drone Pilots Cheer Judge Finding Against FAA. from http://www.bloomberg.com/news/2014-03-06/drone-pilot-s-fine-dropped-by-judge-finding-against-faa.html

Levy, D. L. (2000). Applications and limitations of complexity theory in organization theory and strategy. *Public Administration and Public Policy, 79*, 67-88.

Lowy, J. (2015). Drone on: US proposes rules for the era of drones. Retrieved March 5, 2015, from http://wtop.com/tech/2015/02/proposed-rules-for-drones-envision-routine-commercial-use/

Lynch, K. (2005). A Look Into the Future: Are We Ready? *Business & Commercial Aviation, 97*(1), 46-51.

Marichal, K. (2011). Leadership is taking consequential actions. Retrieved July 16, 2014, from http://thefutureleadershipinitiative.wordpress.com/2011/03/13/leadership-is-taking-consequential-actions/

Martin, P. Y., & Turner, B. A. (1986). Grounded theory and organizational research. *The Journal of Applied Behavioral Science, 22*(2), 141-157.

McAdam, R., & Leonard, D. (1999). The Contribution of Learning Organization Principles to Large-scale Business Process Re-Engineering. *Knowledge & Process Management, 6*(3), 176-183.

McLeod, S. (2007). Maslow's Hierarchy of Needs. Retrieved August 16, 2014, from http://www.simplypsychology.org/maslow.html#sthash.WwEy2JWp.dpbs

Meier, P. (2015a). Digital Humanitarians. Retrieved March 12, 2015

Meier, P. (2015b). UAViators DOCS. Retrieved March 15, 2015, from http://uaviators.org/docs

Melito, T. (2012). *Agencies Could Improve Information Sharing and End-Use Monitoring on Unmanned Aerial Vehicle Exports.* (GAO-12-536). Washington D.C.: Government Publishing Office Retrieved from www.gao.gov/products/GAO-12-536.

Model Aircraft Operating Standards. (1981). (AC 91-57). Washington DC: Retrieved from http://www.faa.gov/documentlibrary/media/advisory_circular/91-57.pdf.

Moelter, J. R. (2002). Effects of foreign perceptions of US casualty aversion on US international relations: DTIC Document.

Morrison, K. (2002). *School leadership and complexity theory*: Psychology Press.

Mumm, H. (2014). Research Study Field notes for The Integration and Harmonization of the National Airspace for Unmanned and Manned Systems.

National Airspace System: Experts' Views on Improving the U.S. Air Traffic Control Modernization Program: GAO-05-333SP. (2005). *GAO Reports*, 1.

National Airspace System: Transformation will Require Cultural Change, Balanced Funding Priorities, and Use of All Available Management Tools: GAO-06-154. (2005). U.S. Government Accountability Office Retrieved from http://search.ebscohost.com/login.aspx?direct=true&db=tsh&AN=18843833&site=ehost-live.

National Policy-Flight Standards Service Oversight-order 800.368A. (2012). Washington DC: Federal Aviation Admistration Retrieved from http://fsims.faa.gov/wdocs/Orders/8000_368.htm.

Naughton, R. (2002, February 2, 2003). The first air raid - by balloons! *Remote Piloted Aerial Vehicles : An Anthology.* Retrieved July 12, 2013, from http://www.ctie.monash.edu/hargrave/rpav_home.html#Beginnings

Ozer, B., & Seker, G. (2013). Complexity Theory and Public Policy: A New Way to Put New Public Management and Governance in Perspective. *Journal of Faculty of Economics & Administrative Sciences, 18*(1), 89-102.

PART 61—Certification: Pilots, Flight Instructors, And Ground Instructors. (2013, 9/27/2013). Retrieved 10/14/2013, 2013, from http://www.ecfr.gov/cgi-bin/text-idx?c=ecfr&sid=40760189a

03dfea0b501608f33820a45&rgn=div5&view=text&node=14:2.0 .1.1.2&idno=14

Passeri, P. (2013). June 2013 Cyber Attacks Statistics. Retrieved February 13, 2014, from http://hackmageddon.com/category/ security/cyber-attacks-statistics/

Paylor, A. (2013). Aiming for Seamless Skies. *Air Transport World, 50*(5), 37-38.

Peck, M. (2015). Armed UAVs to dominate market. Retrieved March 12, 2015, from http://www.c4isrnet.com/story/ military-tech/uas/2015/03/03/armed-uavs-dominate-mar- ket/24328239/

Peck, M. S. (1998). *Further along the road less traveled: The unending journey towards spiritual growth*: Simon and Schuster.

Ponzi, L. J., Fombrun, C. J., & Gardberg, N. A. (2011). RepTrak™ Pulse: Conceptualizing and Validating a Short-Form Measure of Corporate Reputation. *Corporate Reputation Review, 14*(1), 15-35. doi: 10.1057/crr.2011.5

Porritt, D. (2005). The Reputational Failure of Financial Success: The 'Bottom Line Backlash' Effect. *Corporate Reputation Review, 8*(3), 198-213.

Powell, C. (2010). Leadership Primer. Retrieved July 7, 2014, from http://manage-this.com/colin-powell-on-leadership/

Preparing for an Emergency. (2013). Retrieved November 19, 2013, from http://www.pwcgov.org/government/dept/FR/OEM/Pages/ Preparing-for-an-Emergency.aspx

Program Objective Memorandum. (2014). Retrieved February 7, 2015, from https://dap.dau.mil/acquipedia/Pages/ArticleDetails. aspx?aid=d72dabd4-f4f5-4864-96a5-f3357ff50280

Putterman, L. (2013). Overcoming the 5 Dangers of Micromanag- ing. Retrieved March 1, 2015, from http://www.larryputterman. com/overcoming-the-5-dangers-of-micromanaging/#sthash. HOKiJOMR.dpuf

Raelin, J. A. (2004). Don't bother putting leadership into people. *The Academy of Management Executive, 18*(3), 131-135.

Reagan, R. (1993). The Character that Takes Command. Retrieved November 11, 2012, from http://www.wisdomcommons.org/wis-bits/2126-the-character-that-takes-command

Reddiar, C., Kleyn, N., & Abratt, R. (2012). Director's perspectives on the meaning and dimensions of corporate reputation. *South African Journal of Business Management, 43*(3), 29-39.

Roadmap, F. (2013). *Integration of Civil Unmanned Aircraft Systems (UAS) in the National Airspace System (NAS) Roadmap.* Retrieved from http://www.faa.gov/about/initiatives/uas/media/UAS_Road-map_2013.pdf.

Roberts, N. (2000). Wicked problems and network approaches to resolution. *International public management review, 1*(1), 1-19.

Rose, C. (Writer). (2013). Amazon's Jeff Bezos looks to the future [TV]. In D. Mihailovich (Producer), *60 Minutes.* CBS.

Rule, T. (2012). Airspace and the Takings Clause. *Washington University Law Review, Forthcoming,* 426-428.

Saeed Nazari, T., & Nejadsarvari, N. (2014). Definition of medical ethics: dos and don'ts. *Iranian Journal of Microbiology, 6*(1), 1-11.

Saynisch, M. (2010). Beyond frontiers of traditional project management: An approach to evolutionary, self-organizational principles and the complexity theory—results of the research program. *Project Management Journal, 41*(2), 21-37. doi: 10.1002/pmj.20159

Schofield, A. (2012). NextGen Turning Point. *Aviation Week & Space Technology, 174*(47), 117-117.

Starobin, P. (2009). *Five Roads to the Future: Power in the Next Global Age*: Penguin.

Sussman, J. M. (2000). Ideas on Complexity in Systems--Twenty Views. *Massachusetts Institute of Technology, Internet resource, http:// web. mit. edu/esd, 83.*

Team, T. o. U. (2011). *Evaluation of Candidate Functions for Traffic*

Alert and Collision Avoidance System II (TCAS II) on Unmanned Aircraft Systems (UAS). Retrieved from http://www.faa.gov/about/initiatives/uas/media/TCASonUAS_FinalReport.pdf.

Teisman, G. R., & Klijn, E.-H. (2008). Complexity Theory and Public Management. *Public Management Review, 10*(3), 287-297. doi: 10.1080/14719030802002451

Thatchenkery, T., & Metzker, C. (2006). *Appreciative Intelligence: Seeing the Mighty Oak in the Acorn.* San Francisco, California: Berrett-Koehler Publisher, Inc.

Thompson, K. M., Rabouw, R. F., & Cooke, R. M. (2001). The Risk of Groundling Fatalities from Unintentional Airplane Crashes. *Risk Analysis: An International Journal, 21*(6), 1025-1038.

Tipping Point-The 100th Monkey Effect-Critical Mass. (2015). Retrieved March 1, 2015, from http://www.visioninconsciousness.org/New_Age_E07.htm

United Nations Committee on the Peaceful Uses of Outer Space. (2013). Retrieved August 11, 2013, from http://www.oosa.unvienna.org/oosa/en/COPUOS/copuos.html

The United States Meat Industry at a Glance. (2013). Retrieved November 21, 2013, from http://www.meatami.com/ht/d/sp/i/47465/pid/47465

Unmanned Aircraft System Operations in UK Airspace – Guidance. (2012). United Kingdom: TSO (The Stationery Office) on behalf of the UK Civil Aviation Authority Retrieved from http://www.caa.co.uk/docs/33/CAP722.pdf.

Unmanned Aircraft Systems (UAS) Legislation-2013. (2014). Retrieved May 16, 2014, from http://www.ncsl.org/research/civil-and-criminal-justice/unmanned-aerial-vehicles.aspx

Unmanned Aircraft Systems: GAO-08-511. (2008). *GAO Reports*, 1.

Unmanned Systems Integrated Roadmap FY2011-2036. (2010). (11-S-3613). Washington DC: United States Department of Defense.

Unmanned, unregulated & on White House grounds: Obama says

drones need rules. (2015).   Retrieved March 15, 2015, from http://rt.com/usa/226759-obama-drone-regulation-uav/

Warwick, G. (2011). Next Steps. *Aviation Week & Space Technology, 173*(9), 68-69.

Weisbord, M., & Janoff, S. (2009). *Future Search: Common ground under complex conditions.* Surry Hills, Australia: Accessible Publishing Systems PTY, LTD.

Welcome to the UAV. (2013).   Retrieved July 21, 2013, from http://www.theuav.com/

Why Micromanaging Is Bad. (2011).   Retrieved March 1, 2015, from http://www.thesba.com/2011/09/28/why-micromanaging-is-bad/

Wiedmann, K.-P., & Buxel, H. (2005). Corporate Reputation Management in Germany: Results of an Empirical Study. *Corporate Reputation Review, 8*(2), 145-163.

Wilson, J. (2013). UAV Roundup 2013. *AEROSPACE AMERICA, 51*(7), 26-+.

Wolverton, J. (2012). The Pentagon Is Developing Cyber Weapons That Launch Without Human Intervention.   Retrieved July 25, 2013, from http://www.prisonplanet.com/the-pentagon-is-developing-cyber-weapons-that-launch-without-human-intervention.html

Wren, D. A., & Bedeian, A. G. (1994). The evolution of management thought.

APPENDIX B: TABLETOP BRIEFING

Managing the Integration and Harmonization of the National Airspace for Unmanned and Manned Systems

Dissertation Study
By
Hans Mumm
Colorado Springs, Colorado
April 2014

Dr. Michael Hummel, Faculty Mentor and Chair

Purpose

❑The purpose of this study is to explore the possible use and employment of the complexity theory as a new leadership and organizational change management tool, allowing the FAA (and the UAS Executive Committee) to manage the integration and harmonization of UAVs into the NAS.

2

Scope

- Primary focus is on the leadership and management portion
- Technology is only addressed as it applies to the leadership and management issues
- Only U.S. Airspace is addressed
  - Research is further limited to Class E and Class G airspace within the larger whole

3

Situation

- With Afghanistan winding down, the UAV community is shifting its focus from War to the Commercial business model.

- The Military will be bringing home a lot of current UAVs and testing new ones. They will need much more than the restricted airspace that already exists for manned aircraft to train.

- Miniaturization of flight controls and navigation systems has brought aircraft that were once thought of as toys into the UAV category.

- The UAV community has not yet faced the kind of airworthiness requirements placed on manned aircraft.

- Many of the UAV companies are small and medium sized businesses.

4

Next Gen Airspace with ADS-B

DoD 2011 UAS Airspace Integration Plan

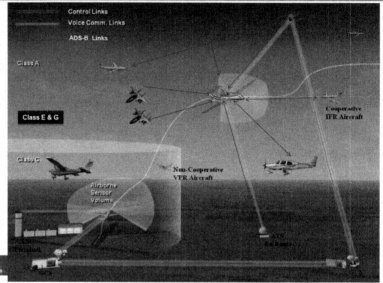

FAA Three Phase Plan

- **Phase 1: Accommodate** – Utilize existing rules and guidelines and apply special mitigations and procedures to expand the limited NAS access currently in place

- **Phase 2: Integrate** – Establish UAS certification criteria, threshold performance requirements and standards to increase NAS access

- **Phase 3: Evolve** – Establish all required policy, regulations, procedures, technologies and training to enable routine NAS access

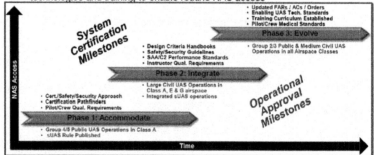

7

DoD UAS Incremental Plan

DoD 2011 UAS Airspace Integration Plan

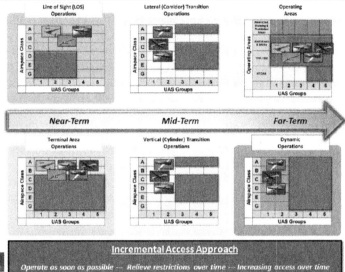

Complexity

❑ Complexity is a: "Set of concepts that attempts to explain complex phenomenon not explainable by traditional (mechanistic) theories. It integrates ideas derived from chaos theory, cognitive psychology, computer science, evolutionary biology, general systems theory, fuzzy logic, information theory, and other related fields to deal with the natural and artificial systems as they are, and not by simplifying them (breaking them down into their constituent parts).

❑ It recognizes that complex behavior emerges from a few simple rules, and that all complex systems are networks of many interdependent parts which interact according to those rules." (Business Dictionary.com)

9

Complexity Theory of Leadership

- ❏ Why: The number of stakeholders and interrelated issues are quite numerous. In addition, the goals of the stakeholders are very diverse.
- ❏ How: Complexity Theory of Leadership embraces a distributive approach that captures the network and uses subsets of stakeholder and issue solutions to create an emergent total solution.
- ❏ Step 1: Map the whole Network.
- ❏ Step 2: Create an actionable Vision and set of Philosophies that will guide the distributed teams of stakeholders.
- ❏ Step 3: Form the stakeholder teams for each issue and iterate a solution with the knowledge from the other teams.
  - – Do not allow one stakeholder to dominate.
  - – Use a point allocation if necessary to break impasses.

10

UAV Integration Complexity Network

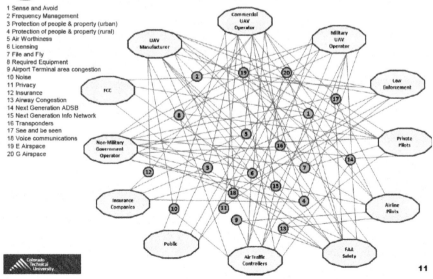

11

Identifying a Working Group

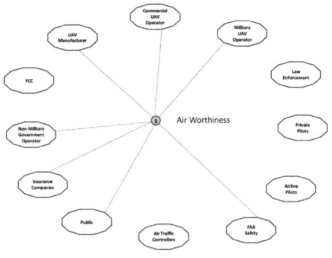

12

Vision and Philosophies

❑ Vision: Create the simplest yet complete path possible for the UAV community to integrate into the National Airspace System..

❑ Philosophies:

1. No significant increase in risk to human life.
   - Those on the ground and those in the air.
2. Experimentation is the only path to growth.
3. Manage any increase in congestion.
4. Use the Next Generation systems to facilitate the process.
5. Licensing should be very easy, inexpensive and tailored to the variety of UAVs.
6. Tackle E and G airspace first.

❑ Goal: Create real momentum in the integration process.

❑ Key Focus Area: Continuation of safe manned law enforcement flight operations.

13

RESEARCH QUESTION AND ANSWER PERIOD

14

BACK-UP SLIDE INFO

15

FAA Roadmap Overview
FAA UAS Roadmap 2013

1. **Accommodation**
2. **Integration**
3. **Evolution**

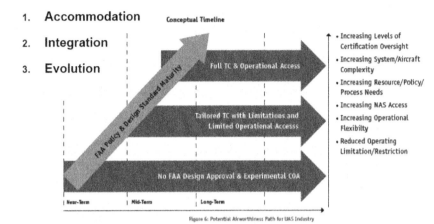

Figure 6: Potential Airworthiness Path for UAS Industry

16

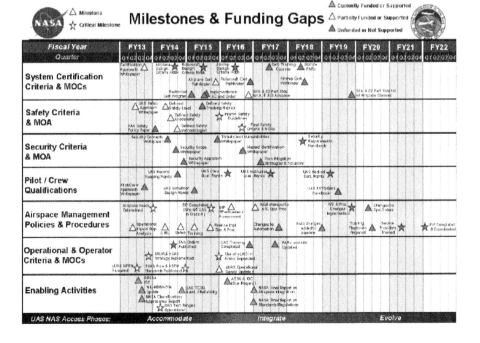

UAV References and Resources

1 - NextGen UAS Research, Development and Demonstration Roadmap (JPDO) (March 2012)

2 - Integration of Civil UAS into the NAS - Roadmap Basis (FAA ARC) (June 2012)

3 - FAA Civil/Public UAS Roadmap (2010)

4 - NAS Access Plan for Federal Public UAS (ExCom) (October 2010)

5 - DoD UAS Airspace Integration Plan (March 2011)

6 - DoD Unmanned Systems Integrated Roadmap FY2011-2036 (2011)

7 - National Aeronautics Research and Development Plan - Progress Assessment (NSTC) (December 2011)

8 - UAS Integration in the NAS Project Briefing (NASA) (April 26, 2012)

9 - RTCA SC-203 Terms of Reference (TOR) (April 26, 2010)

10 - GANIS Working Document - ICAO Aviation System Block Upgrades (ASBUs) (August 12, 2011)

11 - An R&D Roadmap of UAS Access to the NextGen ATS - Vol 1 (NASA ARD) (December 17, 2010)

12 - ICAO Circular 328- AN/190 - UAS (UASSG) (March 10, 2011)

18

APPENDIX C: QUESTIONNAIRE

1. How might the FAA employ a complexity style of change management to integrate UAVs into the NAS?

2. Could the employment of a complexity style of change management expedite the integration of UAV into the NAS? Why or why not?

3. What are the critical leadership issues impeding the movement of UAVs into the NAS?

4. Based on the study's explanation of integrating UAVs into the NAS using a complexity style of leadership, would you favor this normative change if it could accelerate the process of integrating UAVs into the NAS? Why or why not?

5. How do you think the complexity style of leadership could help your stakeholder group?

What are your thoughts on using a complexity leadership model that would allow the UAV stakeholder community to create the rules that govern UAVs in the NAS and the FAA approving them?

APPENDIX D: INTEGRATED TRI-CODED DATA RESULTS

This chart shows how many coders recognized the listed themes in participants' responses. Each "x" represents one coder.

Participant Assigned Number	1	2	3	4	5	6	7	8	9	10	11	12	13	14	15	16	17	18	19	20
1 Participant believes current leadership method is the cause for UAV integration process proceeding too slowly.	x	x	x	xxx	xxx	xxx	xxx	xxx	xx	xxx	xxx	xxx	xxx	xx	xxx	x	x		xxx	xxx
2 Participant believes the UAV integration process is proceeding fast enough or too fast.	xx	xx	xx	x									x					xxx		
3 Participant believes the UAV integration process is too complex for the usual linear organizational and leadership problem solving methodology.	xxx	xx	xx	xx	xxx	xxx	xxx	xxx	xxx	xx	xx	xxx	xxx	x	xxx	xx	x	xx	xxx	xx
4 Participant believes the UAV integration process is simple and straightforward.																		x		
5 Participant believes that the use of complexity leadership theory could accelerate the process.	xx	x		xx	xxx	xxx	xxx	xxx	xxx		xxx	xxx	xxx	xxo	xxx	xxx	xxx		xxx	xx
6 Participant believes that the use of complexity leadership theory would not help the process.	x	xx	xxx							xx			x					xxx		x
7 Participant believes the problem is primarily a leadership issue.		xx			xxx	xxx	xxx	x	x	x	xxx	xxx	xx	x	xx		x		xx	xxx
8 Participant believes the problem is primarily a technology issue.				x													x			
9 Participant believes the problem is both management and technology related.	xx	xx	x	x				xx	xxx	xx			x	xx	x	xxx		x	x	
10 Participant believes their stakeholder group would embrace the use of complexity leadership and management theory to facilitate the process.	xx	xx	xxx	xx	xxx	xxx	xxx	xxx	xxx	x	xxx	xxx	xxx	xxx	xxx	xxx	xx		xxx	xxx
11 Participant believes their stakeholder group would not embrace the use of complexity leadership theory to facilitate the process.	x	x							x									xxx		
12 Participant believes the current set of regulations for UAVs to fly in the NAS is unacceptable.				x	xxx	xx	xxx	xxx	xxx	xxx	xxx	xxx	xxx	xx	xxx	x	x		xxx	xxx
13 Participant believes their stakeholder group is happy with the current state of affairs.	xx	xx	xx	x									x		xx		xx			
14 Participant believes there is a significant pent up commercial UAV demand for operations in the NAS.	x	xx	xx	xx	xx	xx	xx	xxx	xxx	xxx	xxx	xx	xx	xxx	xx	xx	x		xxx	xxx
15 Participant believes there is a significant pent up military UAV demand for operations in the NAS.	x	xx	xx	xx	xx	xx	xx	xx	x	x		xx		x	x			x	x	
16 Participant believes there is little or no demand for UAV operations in the NAS.																				
17 Participant believes the small UAVs will be the most difficult to integrate.	xx	xx	xx	xx	x	x	x	x	xx		x	x	x	x	x	xx	xx			xx
18 Participant believes the large UAVs will be the most difficult to integrate.									x					xx		x				
19 Participant believes the FAA could significantly harm the UAV business with over regulation.		xx			x	xx	x	x	xx	xx	xx	xx	xxx	x	x		x		xx	xx
20 Participant believes public perception of UAVs may slow the pace towards integration.	x	xx	xx	xx	x	x	x		xxx	x		x	x	x		xx	x	xxx	x	xxx
21 Outside group execution and submission to FAA support.	xxx	xxx		xxx	xxx	xxx	xxx	xxx	xxx	xxx	xxx	xxx	xxx	xxx	xxx	xxx	xxx	xxx	xxx	xxx

APPENDIX E: RULEMAKING COMMITTEE PROCESS

The Reg Map

Informal Rulemaking

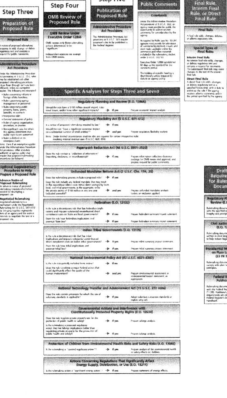

Using The Reg Map

The Reg Map is based on general requirements. In some cases, more stringent or less stringent requirements are imposed by statutory provisions that an agency specific or subject matter specific. Also, in some cases more stringent requirements are imposed by agency policy.

In a typical case, a rulemaking action would proceed from step one through step nine with a proposed rule and a final rule.

However, if a rulemaking action is exempt from the proposed rulemaking procedures under the Administrative Procedure Act provisions (explained under step three) or under other statutory authority, an agency may:

- promulgate a final rule omitting steps three through six, or

- promulgate an interim final rule omitting steps three through six, but providing a comment period and a final rule after step nine.

Also, if an agency determines that a rule is likely would not generate adverse comment, the agency may promulgate a direct final rule, omitting steps three through six, but with a duty to withdraw the rule if the agency receives adverse comments within the period specified by the agency.

Experts in drafting rulemaking documents and computing supporting analyses

Visit us at www.regmapref.com
Also check out www.CommentWorks.com It's a faster, cheaper, and better way to respond to public comments on proposed rules

Copyright ©2001 by ICF Incorporated.
All rights reserved. This document may not be reproduced in any form without permission.

APPENDIX F: ABBREVIATIONS AND DEFINITIONS

AbbreviationDefinition

A	
ADS-B	Automatic Dependent Surveillance – Broadcast
AUVSI	Association for Unmanned Vehicle Systems International
B	
BPR	Business Process Reengineering
C	
CFR	Code of Federal Regulations
COA	Certificate of Authorization
CSF	Critical Success Factors
CTU	Colorado Technical University
D	
DARPA	Defense Advanced Research Projects Agency
DHS	Department of Homeland Security
DoD	Department of Defense
E	
EASA	European Aviation Safety Agency
ERAM	En Flight Automation Modernization system
F	
FAA	Federal Aviation Administration
FAR	Federal Acquisition Regulation or Federal Aviation Regulation
FFRDC	Federally Funded Research and Development Center
FMRA	FAA Modernization and Reform Act of 2012
G	
GAO	General Accountability Office
GPS	Global Positioning System
I	

IFR	Instrument Flight Rules
INGO	International Non-Government Organization
IRB	Institutional Review Board
J	
JPDO	Joint Planning and Development Office
K	
Kg	Kilogram
M	
MPAA	Motion Picture Association of America
N	
NAS	National Airspace System
NCSL	National Council of State Legislatures
NEXGEN	FAA's Next Generation Air Transportation System
NGATS	Next Generation Air Transportation System
NFL	National Football League
P	
PII	Personal Identifying Information
S	
SME	Subject Matter Experts
U	
UA	Unmanned Aircraft
UAS	Unmanned Aerial System
UAV	Unmanned Aerial Vehicle
UN	United Nations
U.S.	United States of America
USAPA	United States Airline Pilot Association
V	
VFR	Visual Flight Rules

CPSIA information can be obtained at www.ICGtesting.com
Printed in the USA
BVOW07s0640030615

402955BV00004B/9/P

9 781628 652024